MW00784880

THE PENNSY MIDDLE DIVISION IN HO SCALE

DAVE FRARY

Printed in the United States of America

Publisher's Cataloging in Publication
(Prepared by Quality Books Inc.
    Frary, Dave.
        The Pennsy Middle Division in HO scale / Dave Frary.
        p.   cm.
        ISBN 0-89024-276-3

        1. Railroads—Models.   Pennsylvania Railroad.   I. Title.
    TF197.F73 1996   625.1'9
                                    QBI96-30060

The material in this book has previously appeared as articles in *Model Railroader* Magazine. They are reprinted in their entirety and include an occasional reference to an item elsewhere in the same issue or in a previous issue.

KALMBACH BOOKS

Introduction

The Pennsylvania Railroad claimed to be "The Standard Railroad of the World." The railroad certainly lived up to this boast during the height of World War Two by doubling its freight traffic and quadrupling its passenger traffic. In the years following the war, the Pennsy continued to maintain its "standard," even when other railroads began to dieselize, use single-track main lines, and yield to competing highway traffic.

In the following pages collected from *Model Railroader* Magazine, Dave Frary recaptures the enduring spirit of the Pennsylvania Railroad as it was in the 1950s. Follow chapter by chapter as he constructs his 11 x 16-foot HO scale layout. Starting with a track-planning model that reflects the rich heritage of the railroad, Dave then explains the techniques he used to build benchwork, lay track, and wire the layout. And you'll even see how easy it is to apply Dave's water-soluble scenery techniques to create a setting that's typical of the Eastern region.

Whether you're out to model the Pennsylvania Railroad or not, the basic principles described here can be applied to any layout, gauge, or scale. We've even included an all-new chapter filled with full-color photos that will inspire any modeler. If you would like to read more about the Pennsylvania Railroad, two helpful references are: *Manhattan Gateway: New York's Pennsylvania Station,* by William D. Middleton, and *Heart of the Pennsylvania Railroad—The Main Line: Philadelphia to Pittsburgh,* by Robert S. McGonigal (both from Kalmbach Publishing Co.).

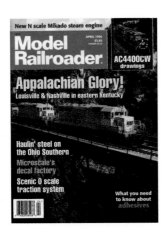

Model Railroader Magazine is the world's largest publication devoted to model trains. Published for more than 50 years, MR serves an enthusiastic and diverse readership. Each monthly issue includes features and columns for beginning, intermediate, and advanced hobbyists, as well as articles and photos showing what model railroaders around the world have accomplished.

Contents

It's September 1950
on the
Pennsylvania RR

BY DAVE FRARY
PHOTOS BY THE AUTHOR

Welcome to central Pennsylvania. It's September 1950, and autumn's approach can be felt in the nippy morning air. Just a faint whiff of coal smoke hangs in the valleys, and now and then we hear sounds from far away – a dog barking, a rooster crowing, the sad wail of a locomotive whistle. These wooded hills are home to the proud Pennsylvania RR, self-proclaimed "standard railroad of the world."

We're on the Pennsy's Middle Division, somewhere between Harrisburg and Altoona, where the perfectly groomed tracks follow the gentle curves of the Juniata River into the Appalachians. This is the route of the *Broadway Limited* and dozens of other high-spirited passenger trains that were sprinting between Chicago and New York decades before we were even born.

Less glamorous yet more important to the bottom line was the steady parade of freight trains. The powerful steam locomotives that hauled long strings of red boxcars and heavy coal drags through these hills have become legendary.

A rich heritage
This is a land rich with transportation history. Before 1850 came several elaborate schemes to move produce, raw materials, and coal from the hinterland to the population centers on the Eastern Seaboard. Canals and incline railroads were tried, but failed. They were no match for the rugged Appalachian Mountains bisecting Pennsylvania.

Ultimately the railroad proved to be the answer. The Pennsylvania RR was incorporated on April 13, 1846, and lasted until February 1, 1968, when it merged with the New York Central to form the Penn Central Co. The Pennsy and the days of steam may be gone, but the railroad is still there, now operated by Conrail. The mountains and streams remain the same as well.

To get a feel for the area I was going to model, I drove from Harrisburg to Pittsburgh in October of 1991. I spent four days watching trains, taking pictures, and sightseeing, looking for areas that were unique to this part of Pennsylvania. I wanted the layout to reflect the look of central Pennsylvania without my having to model specific prototype scenes. I was trying to capture the area's spirit.

When I returned home I consulted prototype photos in books and magazines. I was looking for inspiration and

---

Including how to get started with a planning model

---

information about coloring and weathering steam engines and rolling stock of the 1950s. At last, totally immersed in Pennsy lore, I was ready to model

The layout's features
In the next eight issues I'll take you step by step through the construction of this HO scale layout. It measures approximately 11 x 16 feet and comes apart in six sections for easy transportation. The sections are lightweight yet strong, and the layout can be taken down, moved, and reassembled by two people.

The layout was designed by the late Gordon Odegard of the MODEL RAILROADER staff. Gordon kept it simple, a track plan with the railfan in mind, and allowed for continuous operation.

The track is code 83 flexible nailed over cork roadbed. To keep the weight down I made the scenery from cardboard strips and slabs of Styrofoam covered with Rigid-Wrap (plaster bandage strips) and Gypsolite (lightweight plaster). The structures are built from plastic or simple

wood kits, but painted and changed slightly to represent the architecture of central Pennsylvania.

Preparing the room
I built the layout in a 12 x 20-foot room with a 7½-foot ceiling. Because I was building the railroad for this series and wouldn't be keeping it, the construction was temporary. Most of us have to move sooner or later, though, so I highly recommend these same techniques for building any layout.

First, I removed the old carpeting and painted the chip board subfloor with three coats of heavy-duty enamel. This would make sweeping easier, and I was planning to install new carpet after I'd finished the job.

On the ceiling I mounted five 48" double-tube fluorescent lamp fixtures positioned for even coverage over the layout. Each lamp was plugged into a twin outlet that also served as a handy grounded outlet to use while building the layout. I wired the lights to a heavy-duty on/off switch plugged into a wall outlet near the door. This lighting system was built to be temporary, so I stapled all the wires to the walls.

The fluorescent tubes I used in the fixtures are General Electric F40C50 Chroma 50 lamps. These are rated at 5,000 degrees Kelvin, very close to daylight and a perfect match for daylight-type film. These lamps are available at large electrical and theatrical lighting supply houses for about $5 each.

You could also use regular warm white fluorescent lamps – your eyes can't tell the difference – but they can't be used for color photography. Since I would be

---

A classic Pennsy 2-8-0 H9 Consolidation crosses cut-stone bridge on our author's HO scale railroa Stone bridges and abutments are often found eastern lines. They were built in a time when skill labor was less expensive and structural steel w still over the technological horizo

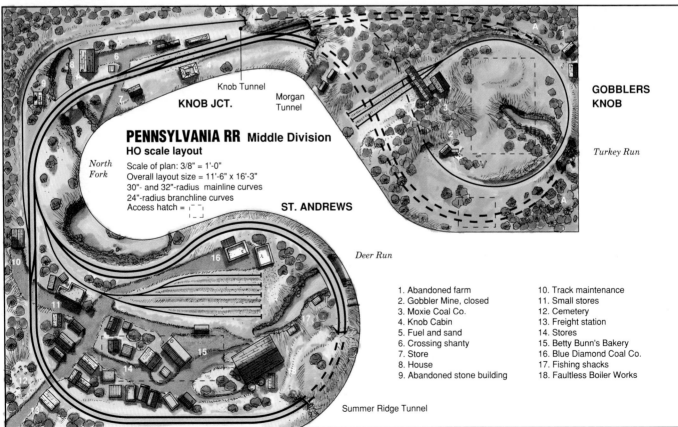

KNOB JCT.

Knob Tunnel

Morgan
Tunnel

GOBBLERS
KNOB

North
Fork

PENNSYLVANIA RR Middle Division
HO scale layout

Scale of plan: 3/8" = 1'-0"
Overall layout size = 11'-6" x 16'-3"
30"- and 32"-radius mainline curves
24"-radius branchline curves
Access hatch =

Turkey Run

ST. ANDREWS

Deer Run

1. Abandoned farm
2. Gobbler Mine, closed
3. Moxie Coal Co.
4. Knob Cabin
5. Fuel and sand
6. Crossing shanty
7. Store
8. House
9. Abandoned stone building
10. Track maintenance
11. Small stores
12. Cemetery
13. Freight station
14. Stores
15. Betty Bunn's Bakery
16. Blue Diamond Coal Co.
17. Fishing shacks
18. Faultless Boiler Works

Summer Ridge Tunnel

Judge for yourself, but we'd say Dave did a superb job in capturing the colors and look of central Pennsylvania in the fall. This is just one of dozens of photos he took while on a research field trip. Books and magazine articles rounded out his research.

The hills of Pennsylvania were interlaced with rich veins of coal, and the Pennsylvania RR was not only a major hauler, but also a major customer. Here a string of empties is being hauled up the Gobbler's Knob branch to the Moxie Mine.

taking a lot of under-construction color photos for the series, it just made sense and was worth the investment to set up for color shooting in available light.

The backdrop

Next came the backdrop (see fig. 1). It curves around the corners and surrounds the layout on three sides. I used 4 x 8-foot sheets of ⅛" tempered Masonite mounted on a frame made of 1 x 3 wood strapping. The frame is fastened to the room walls with 1¼" drywall screws. When removed these will leave only small holes to be filled with spackling compound before the walls are repainted.

To prevent the wood from splitting, I drilled pilot holes for all the screws. The framing extends across the windows and a sliding glass door, covering and sealing them. The one backdrop section that covers the 6-foot-wide sliding glass door can be taken out by removing several screws, as I needed the door available for bringing in the lumber.

I added 2"-wide strapping along the bottoms of the backdrop framing, perpendicular to the wall, to act as a shelf for holding sheets of Masonite while I screwed them in place.

The tempered Masonite sheets are placed snugly against the ceiling and

extend down 48", with the sheets cut so the seams fall on the center of the strapping bracing. I started the corner curves 18" from the corner, which is about as tight as Masonite can be bent without steaming or wetting it. After taping and spackling all the seams and screwheads, I sanded the surfaces smooth.

Painting the backdrop

I primed and sealed the Masonite with several coats of Sears flat white latex paint. After completing the benchwork I painted the backdrop to look like the sky. I'll go ahead and tell you how I did it – maybe you already have a sky you're ready to paint.

To create a lighter look towards the horizon I used two flat latex interior wall paints, Sears no. 125 Royal Blue Medium Bright and the same flat white I'd used as a primer. As all I wanted was a slightly overcast fall day – no mountains and no clouds – these colors were all I needed.

I could have used other brands of blue and do list four others in the second edition of my book, *How To Build Realistic Model Railroad Scenery* (Kalmbach Publishing Co.). However, I chose the Sears color because it's available everywhere there's a Sears store.

While at Sears I also purchased two

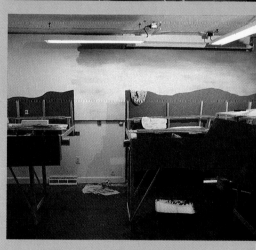

Fig. 1. ROOM PREPARATION. Dave built this MR project layout in his den. First step in building the backdrop was screwing a framework made of 1 x 3s to the walls. Then he screwed on Masonite and spackled and sanded the joints. In the third shot we get a preview of next month's article on building benchwork, as well as a look at the painted sky.

Here's our author, Dave Frary, and his HO creation. Dave lives near Boston and is a lobsterman with many other interests – including photography and model railroading. He's the author of Kalmbach's most popular book, *How To Build Realistic Model Railroad Scenery*.

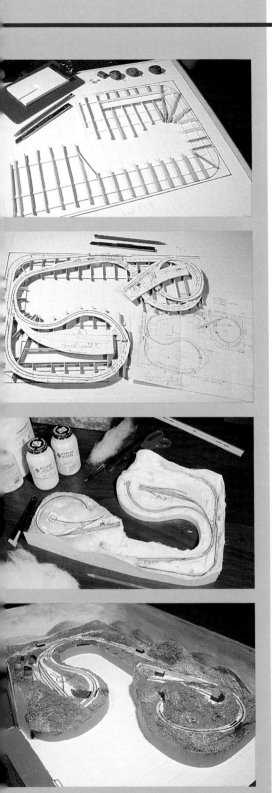

Fig. 2. MODEL OF A MODEL. Dave has learned the hard way that what looks good on paper doesn't always work out in three dimensions. To check out the layout plan he made a scale model. First he cut cardboard to scale sizes and made model benchwork. Then he added a cardboard mock-up of the plywood roadbed. Scenery was worked in with poly fiber and painted with acrylic paints.

paintbrushes, a 3" and a 4", as well as a plastic paint bucket. I used the 3" brush to apply the paints and the 4" to blend the colors.

The backdrop painting went like this: I filled the plastic bucket with water, then used the 4" brush to wet an area about 36" wide. A wet backdrop keeps the latex paint fluid so it isn't absorbed into the dry primer before you have a chance to do any blending.

Loading the 3" brush with blue paint and starting at the top, I brushed down horizontally about 12", using broad, parallel strokes. Next, I dipped the brush into the white and continued painting down the backdrop another 12" or so, allowing the blue and white to mix on the wall. Then I added more white to the brush, until the color on the bottom of the backdrop was almost pure white. I cleaned the 3" brush and went to the next 36" section.

After painting three or four sections, I returned to where I'd begun and started blending the colors. Using the 4" brush almost dry and with broad horizontal strokes, I smoothed the colors together using just the tip of the brush and lightly touching the backdrop.

If the 4" brush picks up too much paint, I clean it with water, wipe it almost dry, and continue smoothing. You don't want to remove paint in this process, just blend the colors.

Once I'd finished I stood back and evaluated the effect. Changes were made by adding more white or blue paint and feathering them with the 4" brush.

Building a planning model

From past experience I knew the best way to save construction time and anticipate problems was to make a ½" scale model of the layout, complete with bench-

It's 1950 and first-generation diesels and steam locomotives are sharing duties on the Pennsy. The PRR's diesel paint schemes were – to say the least – understated, as was typical for most eastern roads. Perhaps dignity was the objective.

work, scenery, and background. See fig. 2. You don't need to make a model if you're going to follow this layout's construction chapter and verse. If you want to study some changes or design a layout of your own, I recommend this procedure highly.

I made several copies of Gordon's plans on a copy machine, then cemented them to heavy posterboard. From one copy I cut out the complete track plan, leaving several scale inches on either side of the track lines. This gave me a miniature cookie-cutter roadbed.

Next, I built the L-girder benchwork to ½" scale using cardboard strips cut on a paper cutter to scale width and assembled with white glue. This solved potential construction problems before I'd wasted time or wood on the real thing.

Also, measuring from the model eliminated waste. I had just enough kindling to start one fire in the fireplace.

I mounted the cutout track plan on the model benchwork, using cardboard pieces for the risers and securing them at the exact scale elevations. Small weights held the trackbed down against the risers until the glue had dried.

A little splicing and fitting was needed where one track passes over another, and I used the second roadbed cutout for that. To finish the model benchwork, I glued a cardboard profile board around the outer edge.

Modeling model scenery

To build the scenery contours I poked wads of poly-fiber fill between the tracks and profile boards. This step will reveal problems in a hurry and help you avoid building an unrealistic layout that's half retaining walls.

Then I coated the poly fiber with two layers of full-strength matte medium,

allowing one to dry before applying the next. The matte medium smoothed and sealed the surface, making a shell that's lightweight yet strong and flexible.

I finished the model by painting the track and scenery with acrylic colors. Then I built a simple backdrop and colored it with blue magic markers. Wooden block structures from a Monopoly set were added to indicate where the structures would go.

The room's ready and the plan checks out, so it's time to call the lumberyard. Next month we'll take delivery of our wood and start building the benchwork. See you then. ☼

Our HO Pennsy layout
is designed to
go on the road

BY DAVE FRARY
PHOTOS BY THE AUTHOR

Use good wood! Those words, spoken by Gordon Odegard, were still ringing in my ears as I set out to buy the materials for this project. Over the last 30 years I've built several large layouts, and with each of them I've made the same mistake – using cheap wood! I had taken knots, splits, and splinters for granted. Saving money had been paramount, and I'd suffered with construction grade boards from the discount bin.

After several days in a warm house, the cheap wood would warp and twist and my level L-girder benchwork would start to look like the framing for a roller coaster. So much for saving money. The little extra that a good grade of wood costs is more than made up for in ease of construction and layout durability. Real satisfaction comes from knowing that after you work hard to build a layout that's straight and true, it will stay that way.

For the sake of portability our HO scale Pennsylvania RR layout breaks down into six sections, as shown in fig. 1. With the legs removed, no section is wider (nor higher) than 34", and each of them will go through corridors and doorways handily.

The price for portability, though, is time. Designing and constructing come-apart benchwork and scenery added about 2 months to the project.

Girders and joists

I chose clear (no knots, checks, or splits), straight-grained fir for all the benchwork: see the list of lumber used. Because most lumber is sold planed, the exact measurements are always smaller than the stated dimensions. The fir 1 x 4s, for example, actually measured ¾"x 3¾".

Because I wanted the framing to be strong yet lightweight, I used smaller cross-section members than I would have for a permanent home layout, ripping the boards on a table saw to the widths I wanted. If you don't have a table saw, your lumber dealer will rip the wood for you, usually for a small charge.

Figure 2 shows how I made L girders. After gluing and screwing the girders together, I cut them to length, taking the measurements from my benchwork plan.

I ripped several more 1½"-wide pieces to make the joists, then cut them to length for section 1, measuring from the benchwork plan and writing the length on the sides to aid identification.

Assembly

I started assembling the first section by laying the L girders on the floor and using a framing square to mark off the joist locations.

After gluing and clamping the joists

Use good wood
to avoid that
roller coaster look

---

on each end of the section, I waited about 20 minutes until the glue started to set. Then I removed the clamp from one side and drilled the pilot holes for the drywall screws. At each location where a joist crosses a girder it's attached with two drywall screws, as shown in fig. 2.

During construction I kept two electric drills handy, one with the screw pilot in its chuck, and the other with a no. 42 drill bit.

A pilot hole is imperative when using drywall screws in hard wood, otherwise the screw will split the lumber. Also, the pilot bit cuts a tapered countersink so the screwhead will be flush with the surface.

For the longer 2" and 2½" drywall screws, I predrilled a hole to depth with a no. 42 (.093") drill bit, then countersank the top with the pilot drill.

Before running these screws in, I drew

them across a bar of soap to lubricate them. This makes the work easier for the cordless power screwdriver and prolongs its battery life.

After adding the rest of the joists to finish the frame of section 1, I glued and screwed a 1½"-long piece of 1 x 2 behind the joists on each corner of the L-girder section, as shown in fig. 2. These cleats added strength and reduced the possibility that the frame would torque when being handled.

Building the leg assembles

Before building the first leg assemblies, I spent an hour trying to determine the best height for the layout. I prefer working on a layout that's high – a habit acquired from years of building models standing at the workbench because of a chronic sore back.

Elbow height is ideal for me, but a high layout is hard for shorter visitors and children to view. My compromise was to build the legs so that the top of the L girders came out 40" from the floor.

I ripped the 2 x 6 fir planks to make 1½"-square legs. Then, using my router and a chamfer bit, I removed the sharp, square edges. I cut the legs about 4" longer than needed so they could be trimmed to precise length after I'd built the leg assembly.

In the bottom of each leg I drilled a 9/32" hole 2" deep. In it I placed a ¼"-20 T nut, secured with epoxy. After the epoxy set, I screwed in a 1¼"-20 x 1½" hex-head bolt to serve as a leveler.

I measured the framework to get the distance between legs, then placed them on the floor that distance apart. Then I laid on 2"-wide plywood cross braces and a Z brace, as shown in fig. 2. (Z braces are

---

Last month author Dave Frary introduced this HO scale Pennsylvania RR layout, built especially for MR after a plan by the late Gordon Odegard. In the months ahead Dave will take us step by step through the construction.

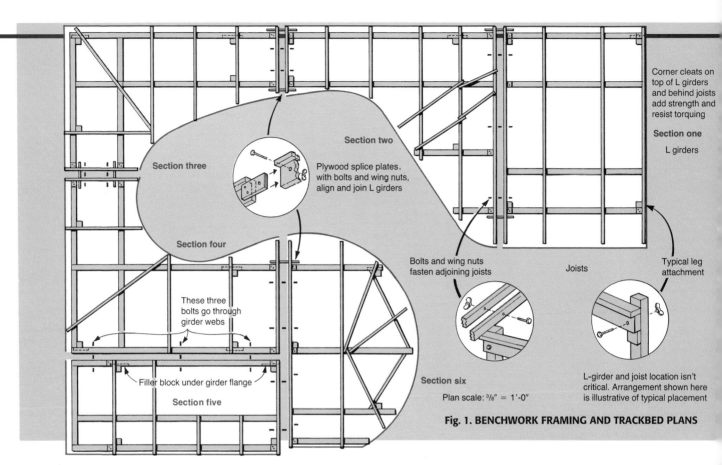

Section three

Section two

Plywood splice plates, with bolts and wing nuts, align and join L girders

Corner cleats on top of L girders and behind joists add strength and resist torquing

Section one

L girders

Section four

These three bolts go through girder webs

Bolts and wing nuts fasten adjoining joists

Joists

Typical leg attachment

Filler block under girder flange

Section five

Section six

Plan scale: $^{3}/_{8}$" = 1'-0"

L-girder and joist location isn't critical. Arrangement shown here is illustrative of typical placement

Fig. 1. BENCHWORK FRAMING AND TRACKBED PLANS

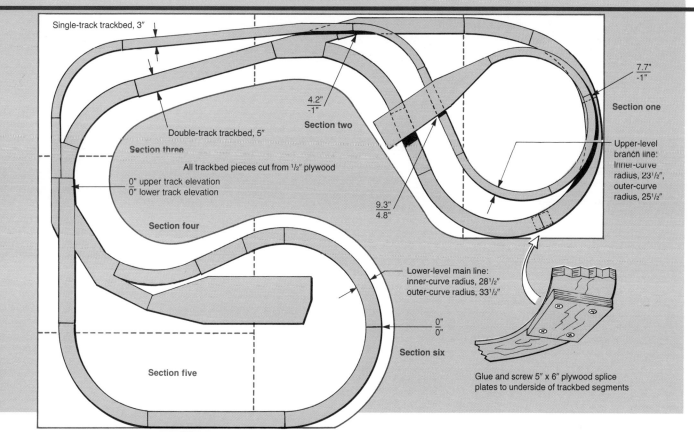

Single-track trackbed, 3"

Double-track trackbed, 5"

Section two

4.2"/-1"

Section three

All trackbed pieces cut from ½" plywood

0" upper track elevation
0" lower track elevation

Section four

9.3"/4.8"

7.7"/-1"

Section one

Upper-level branch line: Inner-curve radius, 23½", outer-curve radius, 25½"

Lower-level main line: inner-curve radius, 28½" outer-curve radius, 33½"

0"/0"

Section six

Section five

Glue and screw 5" x 6" plywood splice plates to underside of trackbed segments

needed only on wider leg assemblies.) Using a framing square I made sure the assembly was square, then assembled it with glue and 1¼" screws.

Next, I raised the frame for section 1 and temporarily clamped the legs in place. I made sure the girder tops were level and 40" from the floor, then drilled a ⁹⁄₃₂" hole through the leg and the girder for the ¼"-20 x 3" carriage bolts. The bolts are secured with no. 10 flat washers and wing nuts. Check to see that the wing nuts can be reached easily from under the layout.

Two ½" x ¾" fir strips were added to brace each leg assembly. One end is attached to the bottom of the leg with a drywall screw. The top end is attached to the girder with a ¼"-20 hex-head bolt, with a ¼" flat washer on the head end and a no. 10 washer and wing nut on the threaded end. These light-duty braces keep the leg assemblies rigid and square with the benchwork.

Where possible I tried to have the hex-head bolts serve double duty, such as holding two layout sections together along with the leg brace. In some places I needed to use longer 2½" or 3¼"-20 hex-head bolts.

After building and leveling each section, I trimmed the tops of the legs flush

with the tops of the girders. Then I glued and screwed on two 2"-square plywood blocks to the legs just below the L-girders. See fig. 2. During reassembly these blocks will act as a stop on which the frame can rest while the bolts are slid into place. This frees a hand for other important tasks – like finding the bolts.

Assembling the sections

For good fits I built the sections in order, connecting them as I went along.

To join the sections I used two 2"x 6" plywood splice plates, as shown in fig. 3. These are fastened to the outside, under the flange of the L girder. Their primary purpose is aligning the sections squarely, although they do add strength.

I screwed and glued each splice plate to one section, then fastened it to the adjoining section with a ¼"-20 hex-head bolt, washers, and wing nut.

Also to join sections I drilled the abutting end joints to accept several ¼"-20 carriage bolts with washers and wing nuts, again with an eye toward placing them so they could be easily removed by someone under the layout.

Making the plywood trackbed

The mainline curves on the layout were 30" or 32" radius, which meant I could

Here we are in the midst of the benchwork building melee. An example of every construction principle Dave used must be in there somewhere. Paper copies of turnouts helped get the trackbed right in switching areas. They were easily trimmed with scissors.

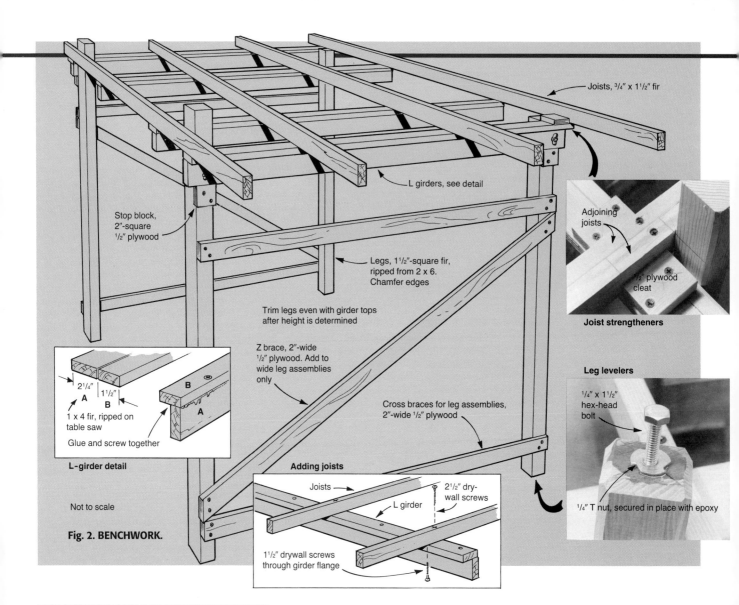

Fig. 2. BENCHWORK.

Joists, ³/₄" x 1¹/₂" fir

L girders, see detail

Stop block,
2"-square
¹/₂" plywood

Legs, 1¹/₂"-square fir,
ripped from 2 x 6.
Chamfer edges

Trim legs even with girder tops
after height is determined

Z brace, 2"-wide
¹/₂" plywood. Add to
wide leg assemblies
only

Cross braces for leg assemblies,
2"-wide ¹/₂" plywood

2¹/₄"   1¹/₂"
A   B
B   A
1 x 4 fir, ripped on
table saw
Glue and screw together

L-girder detail

Not to scale

Adding joists

Joists

2¹/₂" dry-
wall screws

L girder

1¹/₂" drywall screws
through girder flange

Joist strengtheners

Adjoining
joists

¹/₂" plywood
cleat

Leg levelers

¹/₄" x 1¹/₂"
hex-head
bolt

¹/₄" T nut, secured in place with epoxy

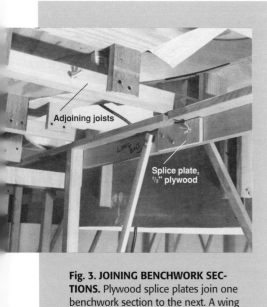

Adjoining joists

Splice plate,
¹/₂" plywood

**Fig. 3. JOINING BENCHWORK SEC-
TIONS.** Plywood splice plates join one
benchwork section to the next. A wing
nut makes it easy to disconnect.
Sections were also joined by running
bolts through adjoining joists.

precut all the curved sections of trackbed
in quarter-circle arcs and bring them to
the layout for assembly. See fig. 4.

To make these plywood arcs I would
first need a template, and to make that I
needed something for drawing the arcs.
I made a simple trammel from an old
yardstick by first drilling a hole wide
enough for a finishing nail at the 1" mark.
At the 31" and 33" marks I drilled two
more holes wide enough to hold a pencil. I drilled two others as well, one at
29¹/₂" and the other at 34¹/₂.". These were
used to mark the outer and inner edges
of the trackbed.

Taking a large sheet of cardboard I laid
out these curves in a quarter-circle seg-
ment. I placed the right-angle corner of
the framing square on the center hole and
drew two lines along the outer edges of
the square, thus making a right angle and
marking off a quarter-circle arc 5" wide.

I cut out the template with scissors,
placed it on a sheet of ¹/₂" plywood, and
traced the outline. I tried to get seven or
more curved pieces on the sheet, then cut
them out with a saber saw.

To get the correct 24" curves for the

upper section, I also drilled holes in the
yardstick at 23¹/₂", 25", and 26¹/₂", then
made a second quarter-circle template.
This template for a single-track line came
out 3" wide.

I also cut three 5"-wide and 48"-long
pieces of plywood to be used as straight
sections. For the upper trackbed I cut two
pieces 3" wide and 48" long.

After laying out these pieces on the
benchwork, I adjusted them per the track
plan. Where the ends of curved pieces
overlapped I marked the overlap and
trimmed them square on the table saw.

Once the roadbed pieces were lined
up, I drew lines along the inner and outer
edges onto the joists. These marked the
riser locations.

I joined the lower-level mainline subroadbed pieces with 5" x 6" plywood
splice plates, first gluing and clamping
them, then adding ³/₄" drywall screws.

The pieces for the upper level were
trimmed, connected, and set aside until
after I'd completed the lower section.

The double-track mainline roadbed is
mounted so the bottom edge of the plywood is 2" above the joists. The exception

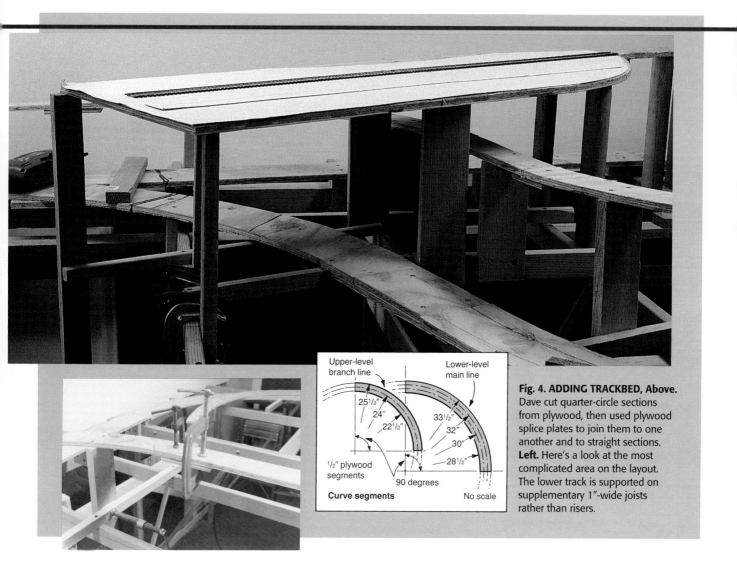

Fig. 4. ADDING TRACKBED, Above.
Dave cut quarter-circle sections
from plywood, then used plywood
splice plates to join them to one
another and to straight sections.
Left. Here's a look at the most
complicated area on the layout.
The lower track is supported on
supplementary 1"-wide joists
rather than risers.

Diagram labels: Upper-level branch line, Lower-level main line, 25½", 24", 22½", 33½", 32", 30", 28½", ½" plywood segments, 90 degrees, **Curve segments**, No scale

---

is the area under the mountain, where the trackbed is only 1" above the joists to provide additional clearance. I started the downgrade to achieve this just below the second-level tunnel entrance.

Adding the risers

I made the risers from 1 x 3 fir, cutting about a dozen pieces 3½" long. Using a small square I marked six risers with a pencil line 2" from the top edge and clamped them temporarily to the joists, locating each riser as close as possible to the center of the trackbed.

Setting the trackbed on the riser tops, I leveled it by adjusting the risers up and down slightly. Once the parts were lined up, I unclamped the risers one by one, applied glue, and clamped them back on, making sure the tops were level. I tightened the clamps and allowed the glue to set for 20 minutes. Then I removed the clamps and installed two 1½" drywall screws per riser.

The risers on the branch line had to be placed to form a 3.2 percent grade from the main line to the yard at the coal mine. I calculated the height of several key ris-

ers above the joists and clamped them in place. Then I set the trackbed on top of these, checked the grade, and added the rest of the risers. When satisfied with their height and position, I glued and clamped them. The next day I removed the clamps and added the screws.

If you find that you've mounted a riser too high or too low, just back out the screws and give it a good rap with a hammer to break the glue. Turn it over to get a clean gluing surface and reposition it.

Some risers had to go in spots where there were no joists, so I had to add some. In general I tried to space the risers evenly, with no unsupported trackbed span longer than 16".

When all the risers were in place and at the correct heights, I was ready to secure the trackbed to the riser tops, using glue and two 1½" drywall screws at each location. The glue adds strength, which is vital for a portable layout.

And there you have it – benchwork that's plenty strong yet easy to take apart and move. Next month my old friend Bob Hayden will come in to help me lay track. See you then. ☼

Products used

Lumber
  ½" plywood, 4 x 8-foot sheet, 4
  1 x 4 x 10-foot clear fir, 24
  1 x 8 x 8-foot clear fir, 1
  2 x 6 x 8-foot clear fir, 6 (for legs)
Hardware
  carriage bolts
    ¼"-20 x 3", 30
  drywall screws
    1", 1 box
    1¼", 1 box
    2", 1 box
    2¼", 1 box
  flat washers
    no. 10, 1 box
    ¼", 1 box
  hex-head bolts (full-thread preferred)
    ¼"-20 x 1½", 23
    ¼"-20 x 2½", 23
    ¼"-20 x 3", 30
  T nuts
    ¼"-20, 23
  wing nuts
    ¼"-20, 30

Bulletproof track
for our
Pennsy layout

BY BOB HAYDEN
PHOTOS BY DAVE FRARY

We've all seen those TV home-improvement shows, where, just as ol' Joe Average Homeowner gets set to, say, install a furnace, a friend who knows everthing about it just happens to drop by. Sometimes, Joe's buddy even helps. Don't laugh, it happened to me.

About the time Dave Frary was ready to lay track on the HO scale Pennsylvania RR Middle Division project layout, I was headed for Boston. Once I'd arrived I dropped in to see how the project was going. "You like trackwork, Bob," opined Dave, "so how about helping me with some of the complicated spots?"

Five 10-hour days later, bent but not broken, I'd installed and tested all the track, though I have to admit that Dave helped considerably. When I was trapped inside the layout and needed a tool beyond my reach he would hand it to me. Tom-Sawyered again!

Masonite bridges

As Dave explained last month, the Middle Division is designed to be taken apart and transported. Figure 1 shows one of the Masonite bridges that connect sections. Dave routed ¼"-deep beds for them into the trackbed. The ones on the double-track main line are 7" long; those on the branch measure 5".

Dave laid the bridges in loose before gluing down the roadbed. Then he cut the cork after the glue had dried and lifted out the bridges.

The track on the bridges overlaps the Masonite about 2" on each end and was glued on with five-minute epoxy. Dave used a razor saw to cut back under the rail ends and provide clearance for the rail joiners to slide out of the way so the bridge sections could be removed.

The bridge sections are held in place solely by the rail joiners. This is adequate, though you'll want to replace the rail joiners with fresh ones if you disassemble the layout frequently.

Laying cork

Dave had installed all the cork roadbed before I arrived. See fig. 2. After drawing his center lines he brushed white glue diluted 50:50 with water onto the plywood, doing about a 36" stretch at a time. Then he laid on the cork strips and stapled them every 3" or 4", with the staples straddling the center line. Once the glue had dried, Dave removed the staples.

Next, he staggered the ends of the cork and used a sharp utility knife to trim it so it would fit snugly under turnouts, crossovers, and other spots where tracks meet.

Careful soldering and filing pay off in smooth running

Dave planed the top of the cork with a Stanley Pocket Surform tool, using long strokes along the length of the roadbed, never across it. He smoothed the cork with a sanding block and coarse sandpaper. A thorough vacuuming revealed one or two high spots that needed more work. This is about when I made the considerable mistake of happening by.

Reliable trackwork

Without reliable track the trains just won't run. It may be possible to build a poor model railroad with good track, but there's no way you can build a good layout with poor track. So I set out to fix Dave up with bulletproof trackwork.

We used Walthers (made by Shinohara) and Lima code 83 track. See fig. 3. I tried to use the code 83 rail joiners, but

found them too tight so I substituted Atlas code 100 joiners.

When I'm building track I try to forget all about building models because the two activities are scarcely related. With track we're out to build a perfect pathway for flanged wheels and a perfect set of electrical contacts. The appearance comes in third to mechanical and electrical considerations. And that means . . .

Soldering rail joints

Soldering is easy, and more important, it's an essential skill for making smooth trackwork and reliable electrical connections. If you don't know how to solder, now's the time to learn.

I used the 140/100-watt dual-heat soldering gun shown in fig. 4. On maximum heat, it's the minimum required for the job. I cleaned the tip frequently with a brass-bristled suede brush and kept the tip bolts tight.

Practice by soldering two lengths of flextrack together to make a double-length section. The resultant extra-long piece may be awkward to handle, but the tradeoff is that we can work on the joints beforehand.

Remove the connecting bars between the four end ties on each piece of flextrack, as shown in fig. 4. Remove one tie from each section, and slide the other three back out of the way. After the joint has been completed, we'll work the ties back towards the joiner to restore the gauging and appearance.

Cut off the tiny tabs at the end of the rail joiners with rail nippers. This makes them easier to handle and allows sliding the ties closer to the joints later on.

The twin turnouts and crossing at Morgan Tunnel were the most complicated trackwork on the layout, so our author assembled them at the workbench. Dave Frary introduced this HO layout-building series in our January issue.

Fig. 1. MASONITE BRIDGES. Dave connected the layout's sections with these bridges. They maintain good alignment and are easy to remove and install.

Slip a joiner on each rail, and align the track sections on a smooth, flat surface – a long plywood scrap is ideal. Now position the joiners.

Apply a couple of drops of liquid rosin flux to each joiner, and fire up the soldering gun. When it's up to full heat, melt a drop of rosin-core solder on the tip, and apply it to the outside of the rails. Hold it until the solder flows into both sides of the joiner, then remove it while holding the rails in alignment. Repeat on the other rail.

If you haven't done this before, you won't get it right the first time. I was a tad rusty and had to practice to get back the hang of it. Once I did, though, the work went quickly, and it will for you too. Scout's honor.

After the joint has cooled, use a few drops of denatured alcohol on an old toothbrush to clean away flux residue.

Fig. 2. LAYING CORK. Dave used conventional cork roadbed throughout, cementing it on with diluted white glue and stapling it temporarily. He smoothed the top of the cork with a Stanley Surform tool.

Then reach for your files because, after solder, files are the most important ingredient in making good rail joints.

The tops of the rails come first. Even if they look perfect, give the top of each joint a couple of easy licks with a sharp (that means new) no. 6 mill file. Then hit the inside of each rail with needle files, keeping at it until you have a flaw-lessly smooth surface. A curved needle file is ideal for this job. Finish by chamfering the inside corner of the railhead so there's nothing to interfere with the smooth passage of wheel flanges.

Solder five or six pairs of flextrack sections, dress the joints, and set them aside. Now you're ready for the really big challenge, which is . . .

Preassembling complex track

Let's assemble the most complicated stretches of trackwork at a work station. See fig. 5. This will allow extra-careful work in critical areas. It will also save your back, as you can work seated at a table or workbench instead of leaning over the layout.

There are four complicated areas: the curved turnouts leading to the four-track yard at St. Andrews, the crossover and branchline switch at Coal Junction, the crossover at Knob Junction, and the twin turnouts and crossing at Morgan Tunnel. Let's start with the easiest of these, the crossover.

Note that we aren't always using the turnouts as they come straight from the box. Sometimes we're trimming them so we can enter a curve or get to the next turnout a bit sooner.

Align the track sections on the cork roadbed, overlapping them where necessary, then mark with a razor blade or dull modeling knife where you'll need to cut them. Clip the rails with your nippers and place them on the layout again to check the fit. "Measure twice, cut once" is especially good advice here. I intentionally cut the rail ends 1/16" too long so I could realign the track sections and mark the cuts more precisely.

You'll have to cut away extra ties and trim the tie ends where they interfere with each other. Once the turnouts check out on the layout, take them to your flat work surface. I used a long piece of scrap plywood laid out on the benchwork.

Cut out the connecting bars between the endmost ties so you can slide them back for soldering, then dress the rail ends with a file before sliding on the rail joiners. Solder the joints and clean them up with files. Take the assembled crossover back to the layout and check how well it fits. It should be close to perfect – and a good deal more perfect than

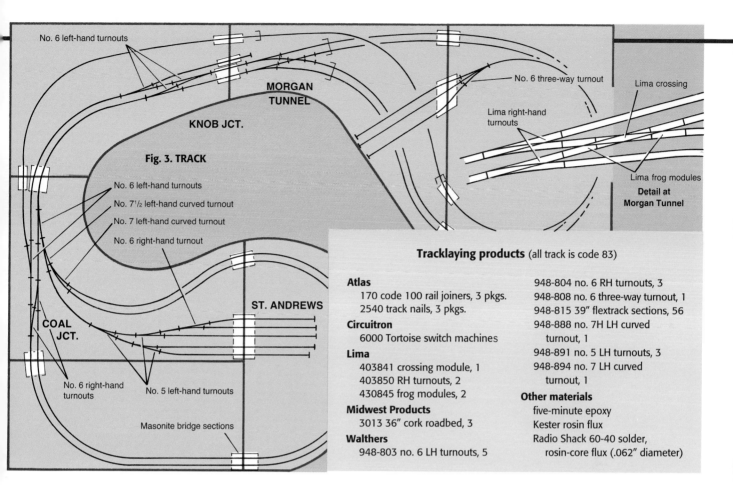

Fig. 3. TRACK

No. 6 left-hand turnouts

MORGAN TUNNEL

KNOB JCT.

No. 6 left-hand turnouts
No. 7½ left-hand curved turnout
No. 7 left-hand curved turnout
No. 6 right-hand turnout

ST. ANDREWS

COAL JCT.

No. 6 right-hand turnouts
No. 5 left-hand turnouts
Masonite bridge sections

No. 6 three-way turnout
Lima crossing
Lima right-hand turnouts
Lima frog modules
Detail at Morgan Tunnel

Tracklaying products (all track is code 83)

Atlas
170 code 100 rail joiners, 3 pkgs.
2540 track nails, 3 pkgs.

Circuitron
6000 Tortoise switch machines

Lima
403841 crossing module, 1
403850 RH turnouts, 2
430845 frog modules, 2

Midwest Products
3013 36" cork roadbed, 3

Walthers
948-803 no. 6 LH turnouts, 5

948-804 no. 6 RH turnouts, 3
948-808 no. 6 three-way turnout, 1
948-815 39" flextrack sections, 56
948-888 no. 7H LH curved turnout, 1
948-891 no. 5 LH turnouts, 3
948-894 no. 7 LH curved turnout, 1

Other materials
five-minute epoxy
Kester rosin flux
Radio Shack 60-40 solder, rosin-core flux (.062" diameter)

---

we could achieve working in place on the layout.

The pièce de resistance is the double-track special work where the main lines plunge into Morgan Tunnel. The Lima turnouts, crossing, and frog sections used here must be considerably modified. It took me a whole afternoon.

After cutting and checking the pieces on the layout, I took them to the workbench. I started assembly by drawing parallel lines 1⅞" apart on a scrap of plywood, then tacking the first turnout to it. Next, I added the other sections, lightly nailing them too. When all the components lined up, I began soldering the joints. (The wiring bars in the Lima sections are eliminated in modifying them, so we'll have to replace them with wire feeders when we start wiring.)

Dave chose to throw the turnouts with Tortoise switch motors from Circuitron. These mount beneath the throw bar, and a wire pokes up to throw the points. Figure 6 shows how to locate the holes for these motors.

At last, we nail down the track

My grand strategy was to nail down the four preassembled sections, then add the rest of the trackwork. After all, the tricky work is the least adjustable, so it makes sense for it to go down first.

Position one of the multiple-turnout sections on the roadbed and push a few track nails through the holes in the ties and into the cork. Sight down the track from as many angles as you can, adjusting as you go. Then drive the nails about halfway in, until they just catch the plywood, before sighting again.

When you're happy with the alignment, use a small hammer and a nail set with a cupped end to seat the nails. Work slowly, lightly tap-tap-tapping each nail to make sure you don't drive it too far and bend the ties and narrow the track gauge. It's better to allow the track to float slightly, with clearance between the nail head and tie. When you drive a nail too far, always pry it back up with the tip of your rail nippers to restore the clearance – this is important.

I like to position a fairly long stretch of track with nails driven about half-way, then sight and evaluate it, before seating the nails for good. You can move track slightly to the right or left by slanting the nail set to one side or the other as you tap.

The glue in plywood is tough, and I bent several dozen nails. When a track nail won't go in, remove it with the business end of the rail nipper and try again. My rule was to try three nails before giving up and drilling a no. 60 pilot hole.

Tips and techniques

Good light – and lots of it – is essential when laying track. I rigged two 100-watt work lights that I moved along as I worked. I also found a visor-type binocular magnifier and a pair of drugstore magnifying glasses handy (what you'll need depends mostly on how many birthdays you've celebrated).

Solder the rail joints just as you did the joints made at the workbench. You'll make better flextrack joints on the curves if you roughly prebend the track sections to a slightly broader curve than you need, cut the ends, solder the joints, and gradually work the track into the final shape. An aluminum soldering aid – a tool used with electronic components – is useful when soldering rail joints on the layout because you won't be able to solder it to the rail.

There's a lot of double track on this layout, so I used a simple gauge devised by Gordon Odegard to maintain double-track spacing of 2". See fig. 7. Another tool that came in handy for getting the track straight was a 10"-long Ribbonrail alignment tool. I didn't use similar curved tools, but they're also available from Ribbonrail in a variety of sizes and will ensure near perfect curves.

If you haven't worked with code 83 track before, you'll find that it's more delicate than code 100. I ham-fisted some of the rail out of the molded spike heads in the ties, but found that I could usually pop the rail back into place with gentle yet steady pressure.

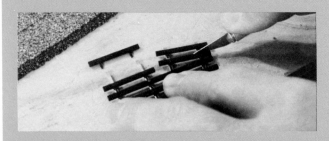

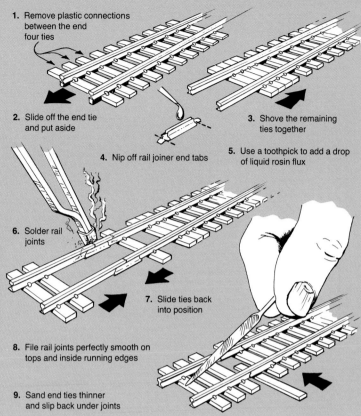

1. Remove plastic connections between the end four ties

2. Slide off the end tie and put aside

3. Shove the remaining ties together

4. Nip off rail joiner end tabs

5. Use a toothpick to add a drop of liquid rosin flux

6. Solder rail joints

7. Slide ties back into position

8. File rail joints perfectly smooth on tops and inside running edges

9. Sand end ties thinner and slip back under joints

Fig. 4. SOLDERING RAIL JOINTS, Above: The plastic bridges between ties can be removed with a hobby knife, then the ties can be slid away from the rail ends and the heat of the soldering iron. **Below:** With this 140-watt soldering gun, you can solder rail joints quickly enough to avoid melting the ties.

Fig. 5. COMPLEX TRACKWORK, Top: Tricky portions of the track were assembled on a scrap of plywood, then installed at the site. **Above:** Complicated track areas, like this three-way turnout, were laid first. Then the sections of flextrack were worked in.

Fig. 6. HOLES FOR SWITCH MOTORS. To locate holes for installing Tortoise switch motors Bob drew lines on each side of the turnout's throw bar, removed the turnout, and connected the ends of the lines. After cutting a window in the cork, he drilled a ½" hole through the trackbed.

A classic Pennsy passenger engine, the K4 Pacific, rolls into St. Andrews. This small town is a shopping hub for a dozen nearby mining villages.

Early on I installed the hidden main-line tracks that run beneath the coal mine and then thoroughly tested and tuned them. This allowed Dave to add the subroadbed for the branch line and the platform for the mine tracks while I kept busy elsewhere.

Tuning up the track

Now for the most important step in building bulletproof trackwork: tuning up the track. Start by picking a spot on the layout and calling it Milepost Zero. Then work around in one direction, checking and working every joint and turnout point. You must verify that everything is precisely in gauge and nothing will interfere with the silky smooth passage of properly gauged HO scale wheelsets.

First check each stretch of track with the National Model Railroad Association HO standards gauge, pulling it along and feeling for tight spots or rough edges. Fix whatever you find by filing or replacing the offending track.

Then run a properly gauged truck over each track section and rail joint several times. I used an Athearn one-piece molded engineering plastic freight truck with Kadee metal wheelsets. The metal wheels are important for listen-ing for bumps in the track. If you hear a click or feel a glitch where there shouldn't be one, reach for the files.

Next, turn off the radio or TV, hook up some temporary electrical feeders, and run your quietest engine – I used an Atlas RSD-4 – while listening for trouble down where the wheels meet the rails. Any snap or pop means there's some-thing to file away that might cause derailments later.

Finally, polish the railhead at each joint with a Bright Boy track cleaner. Then test each joint for perfect smooth-ness with your fingertip. Press hard; any-thing that hurts your finger can derail the trains!

Once everything runs flawlessly, sand some extra plastic ties until they'll slip under the rail joiners at joints and use them to replace ties removed during tracklaying. Make sure these ties are thin enough and won't spring up the joints.

That covers the territory, as they say, though I can't repeat enough that atten-tion to the track pays big dividends down the road – the payoff is years of trouble-free running. Speaking of down the road, next month a different crew will be on hand to show you how to wire the railroad and start Pennsy trains rolling on the Middle Division. ⚙

Fig. 7. CHECKING TRACKS, Top: Our author rolls a truck through the crossing to check it out. **Above:** These simple wooden gauges, devised by Gordon Odegard, help keep parallel tracks properly spaced.

Wiring, ballast, and profile boards for the Pennsylvania RR

BY DAVE FRARY
PHOTOS BY THE AUTHOR

We're ready to see trains running on our Pennsylvania RR layout, and that will take some wiring. Once that chore is out of the way, we can paint and ballast the track and add profile boards around the edge of the layout.

Layout wiring

The wiring on our PRR is simplicity itself. The plan is to run the layout at train shows and other events, so I wired it for trouble-free round-and-round operation with a single train. For running more than one train, see the article immediately after this one, "Cab control for the PRR," by MODEL RAILROADER's Andy Sperandeo.

I chose a Bachmann Spectrum power pack, and for show operation I'll mount it on a shelf at the rear of the layout, where the blue backdrop is now. Andy shows a good location for a dual-cab control panel inside the layout's walk-in aisle.

To get the power up to the track, I drilled holes on either side of the rail and soldered feeder wires to the sides of the rail at the locations shown on Andy's track wiring diagram (which also shows where to put insulating gaps). Figure 1 shows how to solder the feeders in place, and also how to cut and fill the gaps. To keep the polarity correct, I used colored wires, red for the "north" rail and green for the "south" rail. The feeders can be 22AWG solid wire, small enough not to be noticed after the track is painted, but connect them to heavier wires within 6" or 8" below the trackbed.

Rather than doing all the block wiring, I just ran 16AWG color-coded, stranded bus wires from these feeders to a junction point, where they feed to the power pack. The wires are neatly snap-tied to

the joists, out of harm's way, and stranded wire is flexible enough to survive a lot of bending before it breaks.

Where the sections come apart I used Radio Shack male and female connectors to join the wiring. These are six-conductor connectors, and you'll need to allow room for track, structure lighting, and turnout motor power.

Turnout motors

I used Circuitron Tortoise slow-motion turnout motors on all the turnouts that are in hard-to-reach places. Circuitron's instructions explain how to mount the motors, and how to power them from the auxiliary terminals of a power pack. The Tortoise is a "stall motor" switch machine, which means that it keeps positive pressure on the turnout points as long as the power supply is turned on.

On the bottom of each turnout motor there's a printed-circuit edge connector strip for powering the motor and using its auxiliary switching contacts. I found an edgeboard connector made by TRW that fits the Tortoise with one set of terminals left over. It's easier to prewire the connector and then plug it onto the Tortoise's circuit board than to wire directly to the circuit board itself. Figure 2 shows a Tortoise with an edgeboard connector installed.

Painting the rail

After all the feeder wires were soldered in place, I was ready to paint the rail and ties. First I covered the turnout points and rail joints at the Masonite bridges with small pieces of masking tape, then I sprayed the track using Floquil Rail Brown spray paint. Before it had a chance to dry, I cleaned the wet paint off the rail tops with a soft cloth.

> ## It's hard to beat the look of painted and weathered flextrack

The spray paint doesn't like to stick to the plastic ties and there's a good chance you'll scrape some away while cleaning the rail. Mix Polly S Roof Brown and Rust paints together to make a touch-up paint to cover the bare spots before you add the ballast.

Ballasting the track

I used about eight bags of Timber Products Smokey Gray medium ballast. This is a good color match to the ballast on the prototype. So much has been written about different ways to ballast track that it can be a confusing subject. The following simple steps will give good results. You'll need a 1" stiff-bristled brush, a spray bottle of "wet water,"

Paint, ballast, and weathering transform off-the-shelf flextrack into a realistic heavy-duty main line.

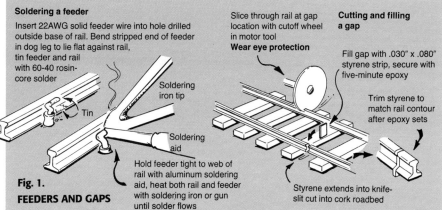

Soldering a feeder

Insert 22AWG solid feeder wire into hole drilled outside base of rail. Bend stripped end of feeder in dog leg to lie flat against rail, tin feeder and rail with 60-40 rosin-core solder

Tin

Soldering iron tip

Soldering aid

Hold feeder tight to web of rail with aluminum soldering aid, heat both rail and feeder with soldering iron or gun until solder flows

Fig. 1.
FEEDERS AND GAPS

Slice through rail at gap location with cutoff wheel in motor tool
Wear eye protection

Cutting and filling a gap

Fill gap with .030" x .080" styrene strip, secure with five-minute epoxy

Trim styrene to match rail contour after epoxy sets

Styrene extends into knife-slit cut into cork roadbed

Wiring the layout and ballasting the track are the next steps toward enjoying action like this, a K4 Pacific rolling a Tuscan Red Limited over the Deer Run bridge on Dave Frary's HO scale Pennsylvania RR.

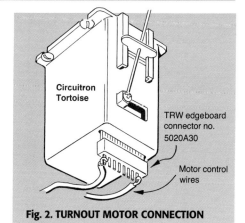

Circuitron Tortoise

TRW edgeboard connector no. 5020A30

Motor control wires

Fig. 2. TURNOUT MOTOR CONNECTION

an eyedropper, and some "matte medium adhesive."

What do I mean by wet water and matte medium adhesive? Here are the mixtures I use:

•Make wet water by adding 1 teaspoon of liquid Joy detergent or Kodak Photoflo wetting agent to 16 ounces of water. I make this ahead of time and store it in gallon plastic milk jugs.

•Make matte medium adhesive by adding 4 parts of wet water to 1 part acrylic matte medium. I pour a pint bottle of matte medium into a gallon jug and use the pint bottle to add 4 pints of water. Shake well to mix.

When you're all set, spoon the ballast onto the track and spread it with your

fingers. Use the brush to continue smoothing until all the ballast is in place on a 36" length of track.

I took extra pains to keep the ballast off the tops of the ties and out of the flangeways between the guardrails of the turnouts. I also graded the shoulders to match the broad slopes used on the prototype. I kept working the ballast until it was exactly right, then I applied the adhesive.

The first step in gluing down the ballast is to spray the loose ballast with wet water. Then use an eyedropper to dribble the adhesive onto the ballast. I pour a little matte medium adhesive into a clean tuna fish can so it's easy to reach with the eyedropper.

Use enough wet water to completely soak the ballast, then flow on enough medium to turn the ballast white. Any bare spots can be touched up now with a sprinkle or two of ballast and another drop or two of matte medium.

Let the matte medium dry, then check the inside of the rail and scrape away any ballast you find clinging to it. This will cause bumpy operation if not removed. After the rail is clean you can

The profile board gives the edge of the layout a finished look, and its green color complements and enhances Dave's scenery.

Fig. 3. PROFILE BOARD SUPPORTS. Dave glued and screwed 1 x 2 vertical posts to the ends of the joists to support the Masonite profile board. In the color photo, notice the double posts at the section joint on the right. The black-and-white photo shows the profile board in place. There was no convenient joist at this location, so Dave attached a scrap wood support to the L girder to carry the post.

vacuum up the excess ballast. The ballast will be stuck in place but still look loose — just what we want.

Weathering the ballast

I like to weather ballast with a mixture of "basic rock color" and "black relief wash." These are two more of my "standard" scenery mixtures:

• Make basic rock color by mixing 1½ cups of "3:1 earth paint" (3 parts water to 1 part earth-colored latex paint) with 2½ cups of water.

• Make black relief wash by mixing ½ teaspoon of India ink, 1 quart of water, and 4 drops of liquid Joy detergent or Kodak Photoflo wetting agent.

Both colors are thin washes that I flow between the rails and then out over the edges of the ballast. They look too dark at first but dry much lighter after several hours.

Other brands of ballast may not absorb wet water as well as Timber Products'. For these you can use rubbing alcohol (isopropyl alcohol) in a spray bottle instead of wet water.

Adding the profile boards

The ⅛" Masonite profile board around the edge of the layout gives the benchwork a finished look and defines the edge of the scenery. The profile board also offers some protection while moving the layout, as well as a place to grip the sections.

I added 10"-long vertical posts perpendicular to the ends of the horizontal joists to hold the profile board at right angles to the trackbed. These were screwed and glued to every joist, with double posts where two sections join. Figure 3 shows the posts and how they support the profile boards.

For a regular appearance all the profile boards should be the same height from the floor. The idea is to make them level on the bottom and cut the tops to follow the contours of the scenery. I took great pains to get the first profile board level and square by measuring from the floor. After that first one was in place, I aligned the rest to it, using a carpenter's level to keep them all the same height.

To see how the first section of profile board would fit on the joists, I made a paper pattern of it. First I taped it in place on the layout to mark the screw hole locations, then I traced around the pattern on the Masonite and cut out the piece with a saber saw.

I found that holding the Masonite sheet to the curve of the layout by myself was a daunting experience. The Masonite tried to spring away from the benchwork and slipped from level. I found the biggest help was a one-hand clamp made by Vise Grip. You can apply this clamp with one hand while holding the profile board with the other. After this first clamp was in place, I added several regular C-clamps to hold the board to the contour of the benchwork. These clamps allowed me to get the board square and level, then drill the pilot holes, and finally screw and glue the board to the posts.

Once you have the first section in place, continue using the same procedure until you've hung profile boards all around the layout.

Finishing the profile boards

The height and profile of the top edge of the board are determined by the scenery contours as well as trial and error. I cut each profile board slightly higher than needed and trimmed it to the correct contour after it was mounted in position. Some profile boards were trimmed a second and third time as my scenery changed shape, so you may want to leave the boards a little high until you're farther along.

I like the color of the profile boards to blend with the colors of the scenery and enhance the finished layout. The paint I chose was Pittsburgh no. 7424 Casino Green semigloss. This dark green is a close match to Woodland Scenics Medium Green foliage clusters.

Trains are rolling on the Middle Division, and we can see the outline of our layout. Next time we'll start on the scenery by building lightweight scenery formers. See you in the May MR. ✿

Tools and materials needed

Acrylic matte medium
Bachmann Spectrum Magnum Ultra
    power pack
Circuitron Tortoise slow-motion
    switch motors
Double-sided tape
Evergreen Scale Models no. 134
    .030" x .080" styrene strip
Eyedropper
Five-minute epoxy
Floquil no. 130007 Rail Brown spray paint
India ink
Liquid Joy detergent or Kodak
    Photoflo wetting agent
Masking tape
Motor tool with cutoff disks
One-inch stiff-bristled brush
Pittsburgh no. 3610 Poplar flat latex
    paint (earth color)
Pittsburgh no. 7424 Casino Green
    semigloss latex paint
Plastic spray bottles
Polly S nos. 410070 Roof Brown and
    410073 Rust paints
Radio Shack no. 274-152 and
    no. 274-155 six-conductor molded
    nylon connectors
Timber Products Smokey Gray
    medium ballast
TRW no. 5020A30 edge connector,
    distributed by Waldon Electronics

With cab control wiring you can enjoy running two trains at once on the PRR layout, and enjoy scenes like this road switcher meeting a passenger train at Summer Ridge Tunnel.

Dual-cab control for the PRR

Track and control wiring you can use on any layout

BY ANDY SPERANDEO

Dave Frary asked me to cover the details of wiring the PRR Middle Division layout. The place to start is with what we call two-rail wiring.

The turnouts Dave used are the popular "power-routing" type. Only the leg of the turnout that the points are set for is energized, a very useful feature that lets you park one engine on a spur track while you run another. This kind of turnout has no insulation in the "frog" where the rails cross. That means we have to put some insulation in the layout to keep the two rails from being shunted together at turnouts, causing a short circuit, and we have to be careful to place the feeders to take advantage of the turnouts' power-routing feature. There are just two simple rules to apply:

• Cut insulating gaps between turnouts located frog to frog.

• Feed power from the point end of the turnouts.

The track wiring in fig. 1 shows gap and feeder locations for the PRR layout based on these rules. If you understand how the rules work, you can handle the two-rail wiring on any layout. Almost.

Turning tracks

The one other trick you need to know is how to handle "turning tracks." That is, reverse loops and any other track arrangement that will turn a train or engine end for end. If you remember that our two rails have to be kept insulated from each other, you'll quickly understand that wherever an eastbound (clockwise) train can become a westbound (counterclockwise), the north rail has to join the south rail. Even if we have insulating gaps at that point, we'll still have a short circuit when the engine wheels cross over them.

There are two ways to turn a train on Dave's PRR. One is to take the inside track looping around the town of St. Andrews. This is an obvious reversing loop. It's less obvious that a train also turns around when it goes through either of the two crossovers, the one at Knob Jct. and the one at Coal Jct. (the junction with the Gobblers Knob branch). If you're not sure that you see this, trace a route around the mainline "dogbone" and through one crossover.

It may look like a train can turn around on the inside track through the Morgan Tunnel, but it can't. Again, trace the route to prove it to yourself. It's as important to see when you don't have a turning track as to see when you do.

As it happens, we can easily control all of the turning situations on the PRR

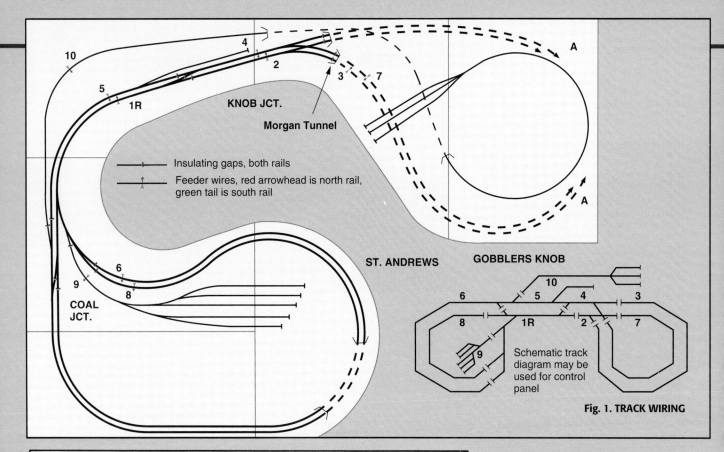

10

4

2

5

1R

KNOB JCT.

Morgan Tunnel

3   7

A

A

⊢⊣ Insulating gaps, both rails

⊢ Feeder wires, red arrowhead is north rail,
green tail is south rail

ST. ANDREWS

GOBBLERS KNOB

6

9

8

COAL
JCT.

10

6   5   4   3

8   1R   2   7

9   Schematic track
diagram may be
used for control
panel

Fig. 1. TRACK WIRING

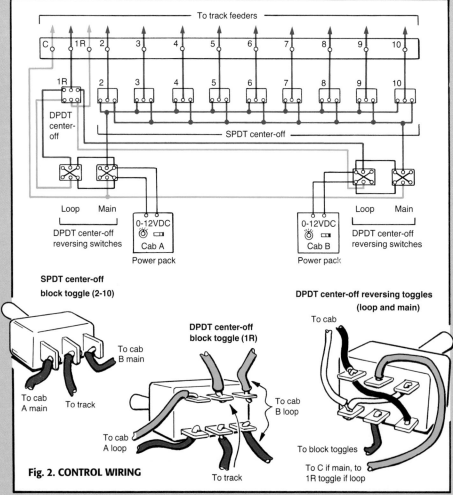

To track feeders

C   1R   2   3   4   5   6   7   8   9   10

1R   2   3   4   5   6   7   8   9   10

DPDT
center-
off

SPDT center-off

Loop   Main   0-12VDC   0-12VDC   Loop   Main

DPDT center-off   Ö ▭   Ö ▭   DPDT center-off
reversing switches   Cab A   Cab B   reversing switches

Power pack   Power pack

SPDT center-off
block toggle (2-10)

To cab
B main

To cab
A main   To track

DPDT center-off
block toggle (1R)

To cab
A loop

To track

DPDT center-off reversing toggles
(loop and main)

To cab

To cab
B loop

To block toggles

To C if main, to
1R toggle if loop

Fig. 2. CONTROL WIRING

in just one "block," the one labeled "1R" — "R" for reversing — in fig. 1. A train must pass through this block to use the loop or the crossovers, so it's a convenient control point.

By the way, a "block" is simply a section of track between insulating gaps. We'll wire the layout so that each block can be controlled independently, for two-train operation with two power packs. But we'll need a little special wiring for the reversing block. Read on.

Block wiring

Besides placing gaps where they'll preserve the insulation between the layout's two rails, I've used them to divide the layout into operating blocks. In fig. 1 you can see that you can run a train around the main line using blocks 1 through 6. When you want to run two trains at once, you'll have three blocks per train on the main line, enough to let two trains circulate comfortably at moderate speeds.

The other four blocks serve different operational functions. Blocks 7 and 8 are both "sidings" where you can park trains off the main line — block 7 is especially nice for hiding a train in the Morgan Tunnel. Block 9 gives the St. Andrews yard a short independent lead, so you can shuffle engines or a few cars in the yard without interfering with a train on the main line. And block 10 makes the Gobbler's Knob branch independent of the main line.

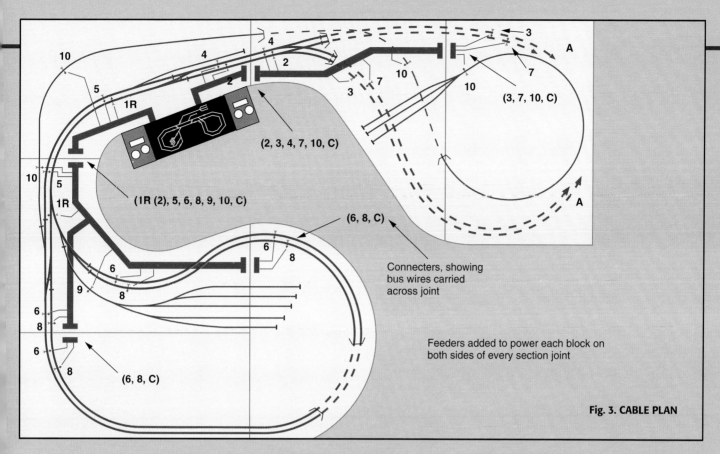

(10)

(5)

(1R)

(2, 3, 4, 7, 10, C)

(1R (2), 5, 6, 8, 9, 10, C)

(4)

(4)

(2)

(2)

(3)

(7)

(10)

(10)

(6, 8, C)

(6)

(8)

(6)

(8)

(9)

(6)

(8)

(6)

(8)

(6, 8, C)

(3)

(7)

(A)

(A)

(3, 7, 10, C)

Connecters, showing
bus wires carried
across joint

Feeders added to power each block on
both sides of every section joint

Fig. 3. CABLE PLAN

We'll control the blocks with toggle switches that let us connect a block to one or the other of two power packs or "cabs," but not both at once. This is called cab control.

The control wiring diagram in fig. 2 shows how blocks 2 through 9 can be controlled by single-pole double-throw (SPDT) center-off toggles. We can connect all the green or S rail feeders for these blocks together at the C or "common" connection in the wiring diagram. This can be a single common wire, a "bus," running to all the common feeders around the layout.

Block 1R gets special treatment. It can't be connected to common, so it's controlled by a double-pole double-throw (DPDT) center-off toggle. There are also two auxiliary reversing switches for each cab. These are DPDT center-off toggles again, but with the special reversing switch wiring. The block 1R toggle connects to the two cab "loop" toggles, and blocks 2 through 10 connect to the two "main" toggles.

To control the layout, flip the block toggles one way or the other to connect each block to one of the cabs. The center-off positions of the toggles can be used to turn a block off to hold a train while you run something else on another part of the layout. Normally both the main and loop toggles for a cab would be set the same way, for eastbound or westbound travel around the main line. Use the reversing switch on the power

pack for forward or reverse movements.

When you want to turn a train through the reverse loop, wait until it enters block 1R, then switch the main toggle. When the train passes from 1R to block 8, switch the loop toggle to match the main.

To turn a train through a crossover from block 4 or 6, first set the loop toggle opposite the main. Then run the train through the crossover and switch the main toggle while the train is in 1R. Use the opposite sequence to turn a train through a crossover from 1R. You'll quickly get the hang of this and find you have a lot of flexibility in routing trains.

Control panel and cables

All these controls and cabs should be mounted on a central control panel. The panel can also include the toggles for the Tortoise switch motors. My choice for a location would be inside the layout at Knob Jct. Since Dave didn't build a control panel, you're on your own here. My book, *Easy Model Railroad Wiring*, from Kalmbach Publishing Co., shows one way to make one and goes into more detail on wiring any layout.

All the wiring inside the control panel should connect to a terminal strip where you can connect cables from the layout. As Dave mentioned, you'll need plug connectors at the section joints so the wiring can easily be taken apart and put back together. You also need to be sure that each block has at least one set of

feeders on each section. I've shown how to run the cables and locate the extra feeders in fig. 3, with the control panel at Knob Jct.

Toggles, terminal strips, wire, and connectors aren't things you'll find at every hobby store. The Radio Shack chain stores usually don't stock these supplies in enough depth to wire anything but a very small layout. You may find a helpful retail electrical or electronics supply store in your local Yellow Pages. Just in case, I'm listing some mail-order suppliers that specialize in wiring for model railroads. Good luck. ✿

Featherweight hills
for our
Pennsy layout

BY DAVE FRARY
PHOTOS BY THE AUTHOR

Now comes the magical part of model railroading. We start adding hills and dales, and those plywood curves that swung out into space start going somewhere. They become part of a landscape in miniature.

This art isn't without its practical side, though. Certainly we want the scenery to be durable, and if we ever want to move the layout, we'd prefer that it be lightweight. Our purpose would be defeated if we needed real earthmoving equipment just to get it out of the house.

When I introduced the layout in the January issue, I explained that we'd be building it in six sections. Also I described building a $1/2$" scale study model for working out the scenery contours. As it turned out, I did follow this model with few exceptions. One area where I deviated was along the seams where the sections were bolted together. In these areas I tried to hide the joints by adding small hills or interlocking rock castings.

The model also served well as a reference for estimating the heights of the hills. This layout has to be removed from my home, so no section could be higher or wider than 34".

I worked from the low areas up, using several sheets of Styrofoam as a base for the flat or gently sloping areas, as well as riverbeds and city streets. These pieces were cut to fit in between and on top of the joists, and attached with Liquid Nails. I also used shaped pieces of Styrofoam as a support for the scenery base in gently sloping areas.

Figure 1 shows how I used foam formers for extra support where sections butted together. I also used pieces of

---

Dave's series on building this HO Pennsylvania RR layout began in the January issue. Here a train of empty hoppers runs up the mine branch. As impressive as this scenery is, it weighs very little, making the layout easy to move.

this rigid foam to frame access hatches: see figs. 2 and 3.

For the rest of the scenic base I used my old standby of cardboard strip webbing covered with Rigid Wrap – but I'm getting way ahead of myself. In Nature the hills came before the tunnels, but not so in model railroading. We're best off to install the tunnel portals and walls before starting the scenery shell.

Tunnel portals

I used Chooch and Kibri portals as they came from the box, with one exception. I needed a wider portal where the twin-track main enters Morgan Tunnel on a curve. To make it I took two Chooch early concrete portals and cut

---

With cardboard strips you can model any shape you want

---

one in two 1" left of center and the other 1" right of center. See fig. 4. I glued together the two wider pieces with white glue, using a framing square to keep the sides parallel. After filling the crack with Squadron Green body putty, I sanded it smooth. The splice widened the portal by about 2", enough for train clearance with room to spare.

Painting the portals went quickly, using a spray can of Floquil Concrete. I let this dry 24 hours, then weathered the portals with a black wash made from 1 teaspoon of India ink mixed in a pint of rubbing alcohol.

When the portals were thoroughly dry, I dry-brushed them with Polly S Reefer White, using a stiff brush. Then I finished the weathering by brushing on powdered pastel chalk. Later, after the scenery was complete, I airbrushed flat black onto the front of the portals to simulate the effect of years of smoke.

To support the portal legs I built square pads from layers of cork roadbed, gluing and stacking them up to track height. See fig. 5. I set each portal in place and checked the clearance with the National Model Railroad Association standards gauge. Then I marked the leg positions with a pencil, applied a dab of Liquid Nails to the bottom of each leg, and installed them. Blocks of wood and small weights held the portals upright and perpendicular to the track until the Liquid Nails had cured.

I glued the walls inside the tunnels, using prepainted and weathered stone sheets made by Trains of Texas. After ballasting the track as far in as a viewer could see, I added a few small boulders near the tunnel entrance for detail. Then I masked the track and sprayed flat black paint through the portal into the interior benchwork. Everything that could be seen got painted.

The last stage in portal installation was gluing cardboard "wings" on the backs so I'd have some place to attach cardboard strips.

Weaving the cardboard web

And now comes the high drama, building up the hills with cardboard strips. Fortunately I'd just purchased an outdoor gas grill, and the box it came in provided about 90 percent of the corrugated cardboard I needed.

Believe me, cardboard strips are wonderful – they'll let you build almost any type of contour you want. On this layout I formed the strips to model the steep inclines and roundtop mountains of the Appalachian chain. Even on semiflat terrain, I could twist and bend the strips to represent the undulating Pennsylvania countryside.

I cut the cardboard into 1"-wide strips using a paper cutter. Length isn't important; most of mine were about 12". After cutting, I pulled the strips between my fingers to bend and soften them so they would be flexible and easily shaped.

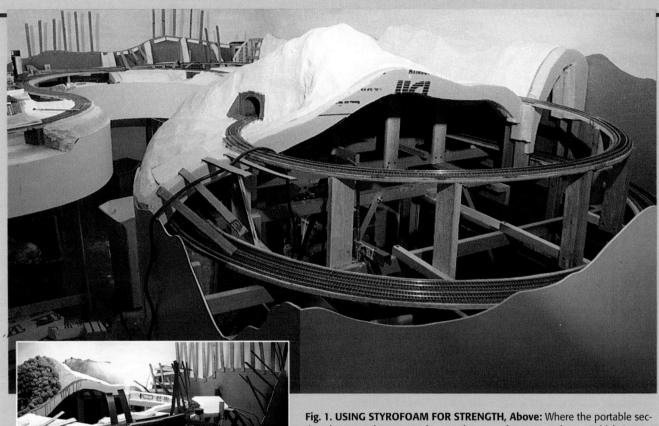

Fig. 1. USING STYROFOAM FOR STRENGTH, Above: Where the portable sections butt together, our author used scenery formers cut from 2"-thick Styrofoam, attaching them to the wooden frame with Liquid Nails. Here the scenery on section one, in the foreground, is barely underway, while section two, behind it, has progressed through the hardshell phase. **Left:** Here's the same area shot from the opposite side considerably later. Dave cut the sides off a Mountains in Minutes stone arch bridge and glued them to the sides of the trackbed. The bridge is a cast foam product.

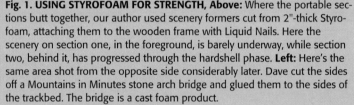

Fig. 2. FOAM ACCESS HATCH, Left: To build the large access hatch needed in section one, Dave first framed it with pieces cut from sheet Styrofoam. **Above:** The hatch itself was also made of 2"-thick sheet foam and finished with cardboard strips and Rigid Wrap.

Working one area at a time, I completely built up a form before moving on. First I glued and stapled the vertical cardboard strips to the edges of the trackbed, placing a strip about every 4". See fig. 6.

In places the stapler couldn't reach, I dabbed hot glue on the end of the strip, and held it in position for several seconds until the glue cooled. Be careful when you use a hot glue gun – wear safety glasses and heavy gloves. I've got the scars to prove that this is not the time to become lackadaisical.

Where the strips joined to the Masonite profile board, I used white glue, clamping the strips with wooden spring clothespins until the glue set. After about 30 minutes the clothespins could be removed and used elsewhere.

I attached the horizontal strips to the layout frame and trackbed the same way. Where the strips crossed I used clothespins and glue to join them. You could also use a plier-type stapler.

Adding the Rigid Wrap shell

Rigid Wrap is plaster-impregnated gauze sold in 4"-wide rolls 15 feet long. It's the same material doctors use to make casts for broken limbs. I cut each roll into pieces about 6" long for easier handling. See fig. 7. If you can't find Rigid Wrap locally, you can order it direct from the manufacturer, Activa Products, P. O. Box 472, Westford, MA 01886.

Two overlapping layers of Rigid Wrap produced enough strength, yet were still lightweight. I started by dipping a piece of Rigid Wrap in a shallow pan of water to activate the plaster. After draining excess water over the pan, I laid the piece in place so that all four edges rested on the cardboard strips. Then I added a second strip, overlapping the first by about one-third. Continue in this way for each additional piece of Rigid Wrap, overlapping each. You can wad or fold the Rigid Wrap to fit in unusual spaces or to fill gaps.

The Rigid Wrap sets in about 40 minutes but remains damp to the touch for about 2 hours, depending upon your drying conditions. After the Rigid Wrap sets but before it dries out, I apply the second layer, smoothing it with my hand to conform to the contours of the first.

If for some reason the first layer dries out before you get to the second, you can rewet it with several squirts from a pump-type spray bottle of wet water.

Gypsolite for texture

On my visit to the Pennsylvania coal country, I discovered that the dirt had a lot of texture. Hunks of rock and coal

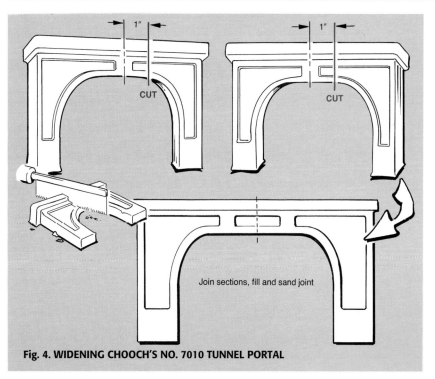

Fig. 3. SMALL LIFT-OUT HATCH, Above: A small lift-out was needed between sections one and two for access to a Masonite track bridge. **Right:** Dave built the hatch from a piece of 1" Styrofoam, then wrapped it in plastic food wrap so he could work the adjoining scenery up and around it using Sculptamold. The hatch's handle is a nail shoved in from underneath and modeled to look like a stump.

CUT

CUT

Join sections, fill and sand joint

Fig. 4. WIDENING CHOOCH'S NO. 7010 TUNNEL PORTAL

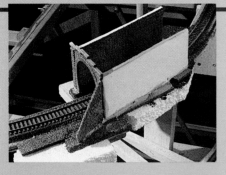

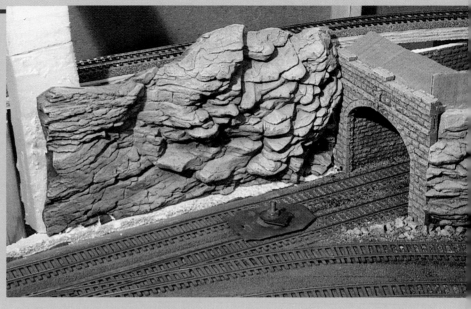

Fig. 5. INSTALLING TUNNEL PORTALS, Above: Commercial portals and stone walls were used to build the tunnels. **Right:** Rock castings for around the tunnel portals were cast at the workbench, then trimmed to fit. Some castings had to be extra thin because of tight clearances. **Far right:** Cardboard wings were cemented to the portal tops and sides, providing a place to fasten cardboard strips.

Fig. 6. WEAVING THE CARDBOARD WEB, Above: Spring clothespins made good clamps for holding the cardboard strips until the glue dried. **Left:** Dave used a brad gun and 1" nails to attach strips to Styrofoam formers until white glue could set up.

were mixed with finer soil. This was most evident in the areas that had been strip-mined and then abandoned. I wanted to duplicate the look of that pebbly soil, so I experimented with gluing sand over a Sculptamold base. This worked fine, and I used it on several small areas. Then, thanks to a tip from a friend, I discovered Gypsolite, a base-coat plaster that combines strength, light weight, and realistic texture.

Gypsolite is a gray, cement-like product made by Gold Bond. (U. S. Gypsum makes a similar product called Structo-lite – both are available from building supply and plaster dealers.) It's called a base-coat plaster because in home construction it's applied as the base over Sheetrock, then the smooth, finish coat of plaster is applied over it. Gypsolite has tooth and texture because it's filled with a lightweight mineral product called perlite.

Depending on how much water you add to the Gypsolite, you can get different consistencies, ranging from a thin gruel for brushing to a stiff mix for troweling. Its biggest advantage is the long working time. You can work Gypsolite for more than an hour before it gets stiff, and it takes up to 4 hours to completely harden. Cleanup is easy. Just a rinse with clean water, and the tools and brushes are ready to use again.

Gypsolite has several disadvantages which I shouldn't gloss over. It must be applied over an absorbent surface to harden correctly. Fortunately, it works well over Rigid Wrap because that material is absorbent.

Don't try casting rocks with Gypsolite. It will sit in the mold for several days before it dries, and when you try to remove it, the rock will crumble in your

Products used

Activa Products
    Rigid Wrap, 10 rolls

Chooch
    7003 "1901" portal
    7010 early concrete portals, 3
    7015 cut stone portals, 2

Kibri
    4101 single-track portal

Trains of Texas
    553, cut stone walls, 6

Miscellaneous
    cardboard strips, cut 1" wide
    flat black spray paint
    Gypsolite, 1 bag
    hot glue gun w/glue sticks
    Liquid Nails w/caulking gun
    matte medium

hands. It's dried, but it hasn't set. No chemical reaction has taken place.

You can tinker with the setting time to speed up Gypsolite, but I recommend against it unless you're going to use a lot of it on a very large project. A call to Gold Bond will get you technical information and a list of chemicals that can be added to change the working time.

Buttering up

One big disadvantage of Rigid Wrap is that if it's rewet or reworked, it becomes brittle and the plaster component crumbles away, leaving only the gauze behind. By coating Rigid Wrap with a thin layer of Gypsolite you seal the surface with a very hard shell. The perlite in the Gypsolite provides "tooth" for rock-mold application and helps to hold foam texture and detail.

As an added bonus, the Gypsolite surface has a uniform hardness. It doesn't absorb paint or glue as fast as plain Rigid Wrap does, so you have more time to apply scenic foam, and you can work larger areas. The Gypsolite surface takes paint exactly the same way plaster rock castings do.

I made a mixture of Gypsolite and water that was fairly stiff yet juicy, about the consistency of whipped cream. (Masons call this type of mix "fat.") With a wide brush I applied the Gypsolite over the Rigid Wrap base about ¼" thick. To add strength I brushed an extra-thick layer on all the edges of the scenery or any place where a visitor might lay his arm.

If you're crazy about winter you can stop now, lean back, and enjoy your snow scenes. Most of us like a little greenery, though, so join us next month when we add grass and rocks. ⍥

Fig. 7. ADDING THE RIGID WRAP SHELL, Right: Swatches of Rigid Wrap were laid on the cardboard web. **Above:** The hills at Morgan Tunnel are well on the way to coming alive. The tunnel portal on the right is the one Dave widened back in fig. 4.

6

Adding rocks
to our
Pennsy layout

BY DAVE FRARY
PHOTOS BY THE AUTHOR

This month we'll add rocks to our HO layout. If you've never tried it before, you'll be surprised – and delighted – to discover how easy it is. Almost all the rocks you see in the photos are plaster castings made in rubber molds. Painting them was a simple matter of spraying on colors.

In the past I've often made my own rubber molds by painting liquid rubber onto real rocks. This time, though, my patterns were foam rock castings from Mountains in Minutes. These 12"-square foam rock faces struck me as fair representations of sedimentary, coal-bearing rock I'd seen in central Pennsylvania. I bought three of these castings, all different, then made my rubber molds following the directions on the Mountains in Minutes can of liquid rubber.

Painting rocks at the workbench

Once I'd made the rubber molds, I cut up the foam rocks themselves into hand-sized pieces. Then I shaved them thinner with a hacksaw.

I painted all the foam rock pieces at the same time, laying them out on a sheet of newspaper in a well-ventilated area and spraying them with a base color of Krylon Leather Brown. While this was still wet I sprayed on a shadow color with Krylon Flat Black, aiming from the bottoms up so the black covered the undersides of the rocks.

After these colors had dried, I misted the castings with Floquil Earth to lighten them. I highlighted the top surfaces by spraying them with Pactra Flat Light Earth.

Once the paint had dried overnight, I dry-brushed the rock tops with Polly S Sand. Then I finished dry-brushing with Polly S Reefer White on just the very tips of the castings.

A better way

In the past I've always advocated casting rocks directly onto the scenery base. This method gave the best results,

but was always a pain. Because you can't see inside the mold, there's always the chance the casting will be flawed and have to be done over.

On this layout I was planning once more to cast the rocks in place, but then I discovered the miracle of Gypsolite, the lightweight, slow-setting plaster made by Gold Bond.

Because of Gypsolite's slow setting time I can cast rocks at the benchwork, then have plenty of time to work them into position on the layout. See fig. 1.

It goes like this. I lay my molds on the workbench and spray them with wet water (water with a few drops of liquid detergent added). Then I add 4 or 5 tablespoons of Hydrocal to make very

---

Use spray bottles
to take the mystery out
of painting rocks

---

thin (from less than ¼" to ½" thick) rock castings. (Hydrocal is a strong tool-making plaster made by U. S. Gypsum. You can get good results with plaster of about any kind.)

After the Hydrocal has set, I pop the castings from the molds. If they break into smaller pieces, it's no big deal – all the pieces can be used.

Attaching the castings

This next part is sort of like tiling a bathroom, as shown in fig. 2.

First I bring the rock pieces to the layout and lay them on the scenery base for a trial fit. I shift them about like pieces of a jigsaw puzzle, fitting smaller rocks with larger ones. For a natural look I make sure the rock strata slope in the same direction and similar faces are grouped together.

If the castings don't quite fit together, I break or snip away the offending

parts with my fingers, wire cutters, or a mat knife. You don't have to be fussy, and the fit doesn't have to be perfect. The Gypsolite will fill the cracks between the rocks with realistic earth texture. I cover about a 2 x 3-foot area in one session.

Next, using a half-gallon plastic ice cream container, I mix the Gypsolite with water to a mortar-like consistency. It should be stiff enough to hold a palette knife upright, but be creamy smooth like mayonnaise.

I spray the area where the rock castings will be placed with my spray bottle of wet water, then trowel on a ¼" layer of Gypsolite. Next, I pick up a rock casting, dip it in a shallow dish of water, and butter the back of it about ⅛" thick with Gypsolite. I push the casting into place and wiggle it gently to seat it.

Excess Gypsolite will be squeezed out around the edges of the casting. You can remove this with the palette knife or spread it out to hold the next casting. I place several castings before I go back and clean around the edges to blend them together.

If a casting cracks or breaks while you're seating it, just push the pieces into the scenery contour. No one will ever notice the crack when the scene is complete. In fact, I cracked several castings on purpose and found they looked more realistic because they fit the contour better.

Any Gypsolite that oozes from between the castings can be smoothed to fit the rock contours or removed with a wet brush. I used a 3" brush dipped in water to contour large areas between the castings. Any Gypsolite that gets on the rock faces can be washed away with a squirt of water or brushed away with

---

The daily coal train running down from Gobbler's Knob crosses the stone bridge at Turkey Run. Author Dave Frary began telling how he built this 12 x 16-foot HO layout in the January 1993 issue.

Fig. 1. MAKING ROCK CASTINGS

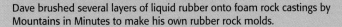

Dave brushed several layers of liquid rubber onto foam rock castings by Mountains in Minutes to make his own rubber rock molds.

The first step in rock casting was wetting the molds with "wet" water. This helps the plaster flow in and aids in preventing air bubbles.

the ½" brush dipped in water. Texture can be stippled into the Gypsolite surface with a small brush.

I didn't always have room to build a scenery shell and then apply a rock mold. The resultant scenery would have been too thick and interfered with hidden track. I solved the problem by build-ing and painting the needed rock face at the workbench, then mounting it on the trackbed with Liquid Nails.

Choosing the colors

While exploring central Pennsylvania I gathered many soil samples and stored them in coffee cans. (If you want to get funny looks, just stop in front of some guy's barn and start scooping handfuls of dirt into coffee cans.)

When I got home I dried my soil samples in the oven, then sifted them to remove the larger pieces. From the samples gathered I selected a pleasant cof-fee-tan color to be the base color for this

Fig. 2. INSTALLING THE ROCK CASTINGS

The castings are trial-fit like pieces of a jigsaw puzzle.

The scenery base is soaked with wet water.

The casting is buttered with Gypsolite.

The casting is seated in the Gypsolite like a tile.

Dave spooned in soupy Hydrocal to make small, thin castings that will help keep the layout's weight minimal.

Several castings can be made at the same time in a large mold. Dave now favors making rocks at the workbench over casting them in place.

project. It was light enough to photograph well and could be easily tinted.

I glued the soil sample to a piece of white cardboard and took it to a paint store. There, I matched it to a chip and ordered 2 quarts.

I also bought a quart of darker earth color and a gallon of flat white. All the paint is flat interior latex. Here are what I used to color the scenery:

• Black wash: 2 tablespoons of India ink mixed with 16 ounces of wet water in a spray bottle.

• Basic earth: 1 quart of Pittsburgh no. 3610 Poplar mixed with an equal amount of wet water.

• Light earth: 1 part basic earth color to 1 part flat white paint and a few drops of a wetting agent.

• Basic rock color: 1 part basic earth color with 3 parts wet water.

• Dark earth: A small amount of basic dark earth color, Pittsburgh no. 7605 Tortoise, mixed with equal parts wet water. I used this for freshly plowed, wet soil and around riverbeds.

I store these colors in gallon plastic jars labeled to show paint type, color, dilution with water, and date. I even like to add a "Shake well before using" label.

Painting the rocks

I painted all the Hydrocal castings as soon as the Gypsolite started to set, about 2 hours after I'd applied it. The rocks don't have to be painted right away, but I find it a lot easier because the painting process can be messy. Make sure to cover the tracks with masking tape before starting.

Even though the foam castings had already been painted on the workbench, I colored them again on the layout to blend them with the Hydrocal castings.

The castings are dry and will absorb a lot of color, so don't go by the color you'll see while painting. They'll look a lot lighter once they've dried.

I loaded three spray bottles, one with basic black, one with my rock color, and one with light earth. Then I had at it. First I sprayed the castings with the black wash, pumping it on until the rocks could absorb no more and it began running off. See fig. 3.

Next, I squirted on enough basic rock color to wash a bit of the black away and add a little color of its own. Then I let the rocks dry thoroughly.

You're the judge. Are the rocks dark enough? If not, squirt on more black

"grout" of Gypsolite plaster is laid on.

A rock casting is soaked.

he Gypsolite is worked in and textured with palette knives and brushes.

Fig. 3. PAINTING THE ROCK CASTINGS

Dave first soaks the castings with a black wash.

Here are the rocks after a wash of basic rock color has been added.

wash and basic rock color, allow them to dry, and check the color again. I wanted my rocks to look earth-gray and slate-gray like those I saw on the prototype.

The next day I sprayed the castings with the light earth color, followed with another spray of the basic black. Several rocks with deep crevices were sprayed with a second coat of basic rock color and enough black to fill the crevices. If you find that you've added too much color, wash the excess away with a squirt of wet water.

After the paint had dried, I dry-brushed the outermost tips of the castings with the light earth color, using a 3"-wide brush. You can hardly overdo this color because as it dries it sinks in and almost disappears. This step gives a three-dimensional quality that can't be achieved any other way. It also determines the final color of the rocks, so if you want reddish or bluish rocks, now's the time to color them.

I waited about an hour, then finished the dry-brushing with flat white, using a soft ½" brush.

Fig. 4. ADDING GRASS

To create grassy areas Dave started by painting the terrain with his basic earth color. After it had dried he brushed on Elmer's glue diluted with water.

Then he sprinkled on ground foam in a variety of colors and textures.

Grassy areas

Where I'd be adding ground cover I brushed the basic earth color over the scenery shell, being careful not to splatter any on the rock castings. If I did, I used a brush with clean water to remove it or blend it in. Everywhere that the bare earth might show I squirted on enough black wash so that some of the earth color was washed away and the black highlighted the Gypsolite texture.

After the earth color had dried, I coated the scenery base with white glue diluted 1:1 with water, as shown in fig. 4. For sprinkling on the foam I used coffee cans with holes punched around the edges of the plastic lids.

I selected Woodland Scenics Green Grass and Burnt Grass mixed equally as the basic ground cover color. I sprinkled this into the wet glue, starting at the ridge line and working toward the track. Next, I sprinkled on a little Woodland Scenics Earth, followed by Spring Green foam from Timber Products. After the glue had dried, I vacuumed away any excess foam.

A second, heavier application of scenic foam was added around the edges of the layout or in places where there might be a lot of wear and tear. I wet the scenery base with wet water and spread the foam around with my hands.

The tips of the castings were brushed with the light earth color.

Highlighting is added by dry-brushing with white.

Then I soaked it by pumping on more wet water. Next I pumped on matte medium until the foam was thoroughly saturated. Some matte medium was actually running onto the floor, which I'd protected with a thick pad of old newspapers.

After the foam had dried, I applied another spray coat of matte medium and sprinkled on static grass. It absorbed the excess matte medium and helped vary the texture.

In the foreground, where many different colors and textures were needed, I sprinkled on more shades of scenic foam, chopped lichen, small rocks, sticks, and whatever else came to hand.

When all this was in place, I wet it and applied dilute matte medium with an eyedropper. Excess matte medium was absorbed by sprinkling on more foam.

Well, friends, that's it for this month. Join us next time when we'll add trees and more details. ☼

Rockwork in low areas, and especially near water, was painted the darkest. Rocks on hillsides are much lighter to accentuate the separation.

Adding trees and roads
to our
Pennsy layout

BY DAVE FRARY
PHOTOS BY THE AUTHOR

The Pennsylvania countryside is lush. Everywhere you look it's cloaked with vegetation in a variety of colors and textures. To model that I needed a low-cost way to build thousands of trees without devoting the rest of my life to the project, nor would just one method do.

I needed quick and simple methods for making distant trees, more detailed trees seen at a middle distance, and 100 or more trees that could stand up to close inspection.

Poly fiber background trees

In the past my favorite material for background trees had always been lichen. Unfortunately, good-quality, realistically colored lichen has become almost impossible to find.

I'd been experimenting with substitutes, fruitlessly I might add, until one evening, while flipping through the Woodland Scenics catalog, I noticed an item called "green poly fiber." I bought a package at the hobby shop, experimented with it, and liked it so much I called Woodland Scenics and ordered 12 cases. From these my grandson and I made about 11,000 dandy little tree balls, give or take a few hundred. Fig. 1 shows how we did it.

The first step in making these polyball trees was preparing the foliage that would go on them. I mixed eight blends of foam colors in plastic grocery bags, mixing several gallons of foam in each. This may sound like a lot, but I'd be using this foam not only for trees and bushes, but also for ground cover.

In each bag I made a mixture that was about 80 percent coarse grade foam and 20 percent medium. I mixed three shades of autumn colors, two shades of dead leaf colors, and three shades of green: light, medium, and bluish.

For the brilliant fall trees I mixed yellow and red foam with a little medium

green. The green "thins" the yellows and reds and reduces their brightness.

Getting down to it

Wearing latex rubber gloves for traction and to keep my hands from turning green, I separated a package of green poly fiber fill into very thin, wispy, chunks and ripped these into smaller pieces, which I rolled about the size of golf balls.

As I formed the balls I tossed them into a shallow pan filled with a 4:1 dilution of matte medium and water. One Woodlands Scenics package yielded 65 to 80 poly fiber balls, depending on how

---

Add polyballs
and foam putty
to your bag of tricks

---

thin I pulled the fiber.

I removed the balls from the dish, squeezed out the excess matte medium, and tossed them into a bag of foam. After rolling them around I shook off any excess and let them dry on a sheet of Styrofoam covered with waxed paper. A fan speeded the drying process.

I used a different foam mixture for each new package of poly fiber I opened, rotating through the colors until I'd made eight batches of colored balls. Then I started the rotation over again. My 12-year-old grandson and I made between 1,000 and 3,000 trees per day, with frequent stops for lunch, sodas, and snacks.

After the balls had dried, I mixed them together and stored them in a plastic bag. Mixing them yielded a random color mix at planting time.

To plant the tree balls I dipped them in diluted white glue and set them as

close together as possible. The textured base had enough "tooth" to hold these trees, even on vertical surfaces.

Weed trees

Most of the deciduous trees were made from weeds I picked in my backyard or gathered while vacationing in different parts of the country. I couldn't begin to tell you what they were. Look in your own yard, or try the dried flower section of any large florist.

I also used several hundred sumac tips purchased from Alpine Arboretum, P. O. Box 712, Alpine, CA 92001. Sumac tips are clipped from the sumac plant, which is found in southwestern California. See fig. 2.

Whether for weeds or sumac tips, my methods were the same. First I trimmed them to a roundish shape with scissors, working over a large sheet of newspaper to catch the clippings. These I saved to make small shrubs and bushes.

Planted as-is, these make good-looking dead trees. For foliage I dipped the trees into the 4:1 matte medium solution, shook off the excess, then dipped them into a bag of foam. While pulling out each tree, I gently tapped the trunk to remove excess foam.

I stood the trees in a Styrofoam block until the matte medium had dried, usually overnight. This method went very fast. My grandson made about 300 weed trees in an hour.

Highlighting and color variations

To highlight the tops of some trees, I sprayed the upper branches with dilute

---

Our author began his account of building this HO layout in our January issue. The background hill is blanketed with our author's polyball trees, with some bumpy chenille pines mixed in. Closer up are trees made by dipping dried weeds in adhesive, then in ground foam.

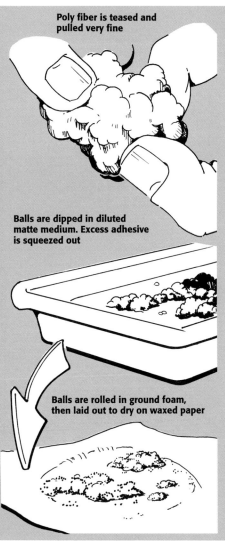
Poly fiber is teased and pulled very fine

Balls are dipped in diluted matte medium. Excess adhesive is squeezed out

Balls are rolled in ground foam, then laid out to dry on waxed paper

Fig. 1. POLYBALL TREES, Above: The trees on this background hill are simple balls of poly fiber dipped in diluted matte medium and rolled in ground foam. **Left:** Dave used eight different foam mixes for making trees.

matte medium and sprinkled on a fine foam several shades lighter than the tree color. Just a pinch or two is all it takes. The effect is similar to drybrushing rock castings.

For variation I tinted some trees brighter green by dipping them in a Mason jar filled with diluted ink. This was a concoction of one bottle of yellow ink, one bottle of green, and the rest wet water. The inks were the kind used for writing on acetate and can be purchased in a stationery store.

I dipped about 50 trees and laid them on newspaper to dry. If you try this, don't stand the trees up, or the ink will run down the trunks and color them a sickly green. These ink-colored trees have a brightness you can't get with foam alone.

At planting time I usually shorten the trunks with wire cutters. I punch a hole in the scenery with an awl, dip the trunk in white glue, and plant the tree in the hole. Wood blocks, metal weights, and paint bottles are helpful for holding the trees straight until the glue has dried. A clump of trees will almost always look better than one or two standing alone. A lone tree needs to be highly detailed.

Three kinds of evergreens

I used three types of pine trees on this layout. The smallest were made from bumpy chenille. See fig. 3. I also used small and medium trees purchased from Shirley's Creative Trees, Rt. 3, Box 338, Marion NC 28752, and pine trees up to 8" tall from High Pines Ltd., 2015 Garst Cir., Boone, IA 50036.

Bumpy chenille looks like a bumpy pipe cleaner and is sold in various sizes and colors in craft stores and hobby shops. I bought 10 light-green bumpy chenilles and cut each into 6 or 8 (depending on the height of the tree) pieces. The bumps give each piece the shape of a tree 2" to 3" high.

I glued these trees to a piece of posterboard with Walthers Goo and airbrushed them dark green. After the paint had dried, I glued them among the poly fiber trees in the uppermost parts of the mountains.

Shirley's Creative Trees are shiny-green, bottlebrush-style pine trees. I pur-

chased an assortment from tiny 1/2" high trees to some that were almost 5" tall. Some I sprayed with Floquil no. 110045 Pullman Green, and others I dipped in dilute matte medium and rolled in home-dyed blue-green sawdust made using Putnam's no. 14 Olive Green dye. The sawdust gives the trees a pine needle texture. I stood them in a Styrofoam block until they had dried.

The High Pines Ltd. trees are the best-looking commercial pine trees I've seen. I ordered an assortment from 1" to 8" tall. They're bottlebrush pine trees that have been covered with a very fine foam and colored dark green.

The taller of these trees can be cut in half to make two. I run them through my hand just before planting to give them a scruffier appearance.

Fun with foam putty

For this layout I developed a way to place ground cover where it doesn't want to go. I call the material I used "foam putty," and here's the recipe:

Start with a tuna can full of scenery foam, as shown in fig. 4. Add just enough

**Fig. 2. WEED TREES,
Left:** Dave's grandson, Chris Genest, made hundreds of trees for the layout, most from weeds. **Below:** These arboreal beauties were made by dipping the weeds in matte medium, then in ground foam.

Dried weed tree trunks are dipped in diluted matte medium

Trees are dipped in ground foam to add foliage

**Fig. 3. PINE TREES,
Above:** Bumpy chenille is available in craft stores and makes good background pine trees. **Right:** All the taller pine trees on the layout were purchased from High Pines Ltd. The only change Dave made was painting the trunks dark brown.

Fig. 4. FOAM PUTTY, Above: Dave mixes ground foam with matte medium to about the consistency of oatmeal. **Right:** He spots it on the sides of rock faces, under overhangs, and anywhere weeds and vines might grow.

Fig. 5. BUILDING ROADS, Above left: Dave began by cutting 3/16" foam core board and gluing it over the Styrofoam sub-base. **Above right:** He worked the roads into the ground with Sculptamold, then painted them with a black primer to seal them. **Far left:** After painting the roads with diluted white glue (1:1), Dave sprinkled on fine sand. **Left:** He painted the roads dark gray.

Fig. 6. POOR MAN'S DETAIL, Top: After the detail is in place, Dave sprays it with wet water to reduce any surface tension. **Above:** The last step is to flow on diluted matte medium. Dave prefers a large, paint-mixing eyedropper for the applicator.

Here's a sneak preview of next month's subject, bridges and water. There's less to this bridge than you might think. Dave just glues the plate girder sides to his plywood trackbed.

dilute (4:1) matte medium to hold the foam together. I like it thick enough so I can barely squeeze out the liquid. There's no formula for mixing this stuff; just add medium until you can stir it with a stick and it will hold together.

I apply the foam putty with a small spatula or my fingers, using it around rock castings, on buildings, or anyplace I need the look of creeping vines or large, sprawling clumps of weeds or undergrowth.

The trick when applying the foam is not to compact it. Leave it as loose and ragged-looking as possible. If you trowel it flat by mistake, you can flick parts of it up with the tip of the spatula. I allow it to dry overnight before adding more foam over it or adding other scenery next to it. When the foam putty is wet it will look milky, but it'll look fine once it has dried.

I tried mixing white glue (1:1) with foam and got a putty with more sticking power. This I used under overhanging surfaces where I needed a great deal of vegetation in an impossible place.

In another experiment I mixed foam with thinned liquid latex, the stuff used to make rock molds, diluting the rubber 3:1 with water. I added enough liquid rubber to the foam to make a dough. I spread it on a window screen supported over sheets of newspaper to catch

the drips. A fan helped with the drying.

The result is something close to Woodland Scenics scenery clusters. I tried using fine, medium, and coarse foam, and found the coarse foam held together better than the others. The advantage of making your own clusters is that you get to choose the texture and colors to fit your layout.

Building the roads

The base for most of the roads was ³/₁₆"-thick foam core board, as shown in fig. 5. After gluing the board in place and working the scenery contours up to the edges with Sculptamold, I sealed the surface with a couple coats of the basic earth color.

Once the paint had dried, I brushed on white glue and sprinkled on very fine sand, using a tea strainer. The trick is to lightly tap the side of the strainer to get even coverage.

The color of the sand didn't matter because it would be painted, so I got rid of a lot of old, brightly colored stuff I'd never have used otherwise. After the glue had dried overnight, I soaked the sand with 4:1 matte medium applied with a spray bottle.

Once the glue had dried, I painted the road with a tarmac color made from 3 parts Flat Black latex paint, 2 parts Titanium White, 1 part Raw Sienna, and

enough wet water to double the volume. I mixed a lot of this color and stored it in a screw-top jar. While brushing it on the roads I found that the colors separated slightly on the surface, producing some gray/black, some earth/black, and a mixture of all these colors. This was all to the good, adding to the realism.

The results looked good but were still a little too black, so after the paint had dried, I weathered the road with a wash made from 2 parts Polly S Flat Black and 3 parts Concrete diluted with enough wet water so it would flow easily. I also mixed several other variations of this wash to make patches and seams in the roads. I finished by adding fresh tar seams and patches with a fine-tipped black Magic Marker.

Detailing the scenery

I finished the scenery with lots of what I call "poor man's detail." See fig. 6. This includes scrap piles of scale lumber, stones, bits of lichen, cast-plaster tree stumps, and rusted leftovers from plastic kits.

The weeds are from Timber Products' Wild Weeds. These are lengths of colored fibers that I cut into short bunches and glued in holes.

Well, that's more than enough to keep you busy until next time, when the subject will be water and bridges. ☼

Adding bridges and water
to our
Pennsy layout

BY DAVE FRARY
PHOTOS BY THE AUTHOR

The bridges on this HO layout were modeled loosely after several I saw while driving through central Pennsylvania. I wanted them to look right, but I also wanted to build them quickly from available kits.

In every case I cemented the bridge sides directly to the plywood trackbed. The big advantage of this type of construction is that the roadbed and track are never cut or otherwise tampered with. The layout remains quite strong, and that was desirable in this case because the railroad was designed to be portable.

Getting started

Step 1 was trimming the trackbed sides to accept the bridge sides. At each bridge location I scribed a line on either side of the cork roadbed, parallel to its edges and even with the outer edge of the National Model Railroad Association standards gauge. This line falls about 1/4" beyond the outer edges of the cork roadbed. Using a saber saw, I cut off the excess trackbed. Then I sanded the edges smooth.

The next step was to paint the underside of the plywood trackbed flat black to disguise the lack of detail. After the paint had dried, I glued prepainted and weathered Chooch bridge piers to each end of the underside of the trackbed, applying Liquid Nails to the tops and wedging them in place with slivers of wood jammed in at the bottoms.

After the glue had dried, I removed the wedges and cut pieces of basswood to fit between the bottoms of the piers and the river bottom. These I painted

with equal parts Polly S Earth and Reefer White to represent concrete footings. See fig. 1.

Plate girder bridges

Two of the bridges are plate girder types I built using pieces of Central Valley bridge kits, and cutting and splicing the girders long enough so that each side extended to the rear edge of the supporting pier. All four bridge sides are different lengths because the bridges are curved, and one bridge span on each bridge is shorter than the other.

To modify the girders, I cut with a razor saw on the plate seams and added or removed plates as needed to get the sides the right lengths. I glued the plates together with liquid styrene cement and added the top plates and end caps. The sides were primed with Floquil Grimy Black, using a spray can. The next day I drybrushed the rivet heads and seams with Polly S Reefer White and weathered the sides with black, earth, and rust-colored chalk powder.

I glued the first bridge side to the trackbed with five-minute epoxy, aligning the bottom of the girder with the bottom of the trackbed and using clamps to hold the side in place until the glue dried. I attached the second side in the same manner, then ballasted the track out to the girders.

Building the stone bridge

The early PRR construction engineers replaced most of the very early wood bridges with stone bridges, safer and

The cast-foam bridge by Mountains in Minutes is easy to cut up and rearrange

more durable than wood or iron. Many of these stone bridges are still in use 100 years later.

I knew that a stone bridge would look great on this layout, but the only model readily available that looked similar to several bridges I saw in Pennsylvania was the Mountains in Minutes stone viaduct. This model is made from expanded foam and is only wide enough for one straight track. I wanted to use it on a curved two-track main line, so some alterations were called for. I thought about the problem and decided I'd try the same approach I used with

the plate girder bridges, applying the bridge to the sides of the trackbed.

Using a hacksaw blade (but not the saw), I cut the bridge into the pieces shown in fig. 2. Then I glued the two front pieces together at the center, bracing the back with a piece of stripwood. Next, I glued the arch interiors to the rear of the front.

I painted the pieces with a dark gray latex paint. After the paint had dried, I sprayed on a black wash and laid them flat to dry. The following day I dry-brushed the bridge with Reefer White and added weathering with green,

brown, and gray chalk powder.

I installed the pieces with five-minute epoxy, spreading it on with a tongue depressor and using clamps. Then, using five-minute epoxy again, I added the arch interiors and the rear side of the bridge. I found that I had to cut the rear section in half lengthwise, parallel to the top, to get it to fit properly.

The stones on the center seam of the front didn't quite line up, so I hid them behind a large vine.

I brought the rock castings up to the edges of the bridge, trying to make it look like the construction engineers

This series on building an HO scale version of the Pennsylvania RR began in our January issue. Here a classic Pennsy K4 Pacific rolls across a bridge made using the girders from two Central Valley plate girder bridge kits. The leftovers provided enough material for a second bridge.

blasted away only enough rock so that the bridge would fit.

Modeling the water

I wanted the track to look as though it followed the river, just as the prototype follows the Juniata, although I did

Fig. 1. RIVER BOTTOM INSTALLATION, Above: Sheet Styrofoam was used for the river bottoms. Later the Chooch abutments were glued to the bottom of the trackbed.
Left: Have you checked the clamp department at your hardware store lately? New types are available that make clamping jobs much easier.

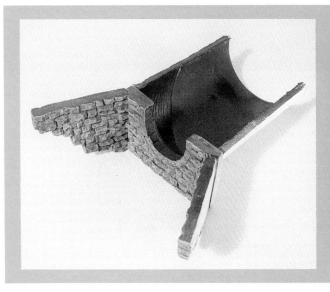

Fig. 2. INSTALLING CULVERTS. Since we want to include lots of other features, rivers don't always have a good place to go on model railroads. One good trick is to take them underground, using culverts. Dave used part of a cardboard mailing tube to make a culvert liner.

exaggerate the height of the banks and the size of the rock faces to get a more dramatic effect.

One of the easiest ways to model water is with Enviro-Tex Lite, a two-part self-leveling epoxy. Its big advantage is having little smell. It's easy to use and produces reliable, consistent results.

On two stretches of the river there was no logical place for the water to go. One river could have exited through the back of the scenery, but would have been hard to reach and even harder to work on. On the other river section, the water would have run across two layout joints and been difficult to hide. I solved both problems by flowing the river into Chooch stone culverts, painting and placing these before the rough scenery was in place. I glued 1" x 3" cardboard tabs to the rear edges of the culverts for attaching the cardboard strips, as shown in fig. 3.

I brought the rough scenery down to the river bottom to form the banks. Then I added rock castings, choosing and fitting them to look as if the water had eroded most of them away. Between the castings I smoothed the Gypsolite to look as though the water had washed away the loose gravel.

I troweled Gypsolite under the concrete bridge footings and along the sides of the banks, adding it anywhere there was a gap or hole to fill. I was careful to seal all the holes, no matter how small, as the Enviro-Tex will find the smallest pinhole and leak out of the riverbed.

Detailing the river bottoms

Next I painted the river bottom with flat black latex paint.

Along the banks I sprinkled loose rocks made from scrap plaster, sprinkling the largest rocks first and pushing them into position with my fingers. Over these I sprinkled finer rocks and finished with rocks not much larger than grains of coarse sand. Fine sand was added where I wanted sandbars or beaches.

I pushed the rocks and sand from unwanted areas with a wide brush. Once everything was the way I wanted it, I sprayed the rocks with wet water and applied diluted matte medium to bond the materials in place.

After the medium had dried, I painted the rocks and sand areas again with the basic earth color, making no attempt to blend this with the black. In several areas I glued clusters of Woodland Scenics wild weeds to represent duck grass.

To feather the sandbar and rocks into the deep river bottom, I used an airbrush, first spraying on basic earth, then a mixture of equal parts basic earth and

Fig. 3. THE STONE BRIDGE. Dave performed radical surgery on a Mountains in Minutes foam bridge so he could work it into the layout. The drawing shows how it all went back together. The vine down the center of the front hides the seam. Lots of crushed plaster rubble was placed around the bridge footings to simulate rocks eroded by the rapid flowing water. The rear of the bridge is almost hidden by the hill.

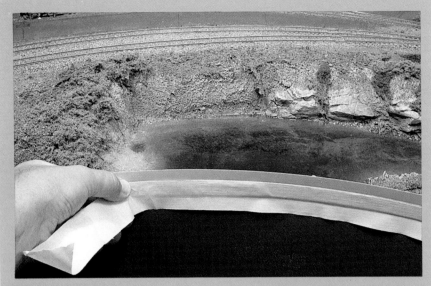

Fig. 4. MODELING WATER, Above: Dave is pulling off the masking tape used to secure a styrene dam to the side of the layout. The water is Enviro-Tex Lite, a two-part epoxy. **Left:** Dave built the waterfall by gluing thin strips of acetate to the top and bottom of the rock castings and pouring Enviro-Tex Lite over them. Wisps of cotton balls were used to model mist.

flat black. I finished the job with flat black in the center of the stream.

I used the earth color to simulate the shallow areas, the earth and black mixture for the deeper areas, and the pure black for the deepest parts. I sprayed these in the direction the water would flow to give the illusion of fast-moving water. To finish I drybrushed the tops of all the rocks with white. For detail I glued sticks and pieces of wood behind rocks and in other places where the current would deposit them.

Products used

Central Valley
    1903 plate girder bridges, 2

Chooch
    7028 bridge abutments, 4
    7033 stone culverts, 2

Enviro-Tex Lite
    2-quart size

Mountains in Minutes
    1827 bridge

Preparing to pour

To prepare for pouring the water I first built a dam along the front edge of the layout to contain the Enviro-Tex. See fig. 4. I began by waxing the profile board with paste wax. This seals the Masonite surface, preventing the epoxy from sticking to it, and allows the tape that holds the dam to be removed easily. I used the paste wax I had on hand – it was made to wax a fiber-glass boat – but any paste wax will work.

For the dams themselves I cut four 2" x 18" strips of .025" styrene. I waxed them, then taped them to the front of the layout with 2"-wide masking tape so they extended ½" above the water surface. In several places where the strips

didn't fit snugly against the profile boards, I sealed the gaps with drops of white glue. One larger gap I filled with a bead of modeling clay, spreading it in the crack with a toothpick.

Pouring in layers

I mixed the Enviro-Tex Lite in a disposable plastic cup, following the manufacturer's recommendations and stirring with a wooden tongue depressor with one end squared to fit flush against the bottom of the cup.

The water was built up in three layers, each being allowed to set before the next was poured. I applied the first layer thinly, just covering the bottom and brushing it into all the places where water should be. This thin layer seals the surface and secures all the rocks and stones that may have worked loose. It's also the test layer to make sure no pinholes are present.

If you find any holes, plug them with

whatever is at hand. I've used small rocks or sticks, bits of detail, and even a wad of modeling clay pushed in from underneath. After the first layer has hardened, you can fill any additional pinholes with a dab of five-minute epoxy.

The second and third layers add depth, getting the thickness up to about 1/2". After the third layer has hardened overnight, you can remove the dam.

You can add texture to the surface, if you have the patience. Wait until the epoxy gets to the consistency of chewy bubble gum, then pick and lift it with the tip of an awl, stick, or pin. It will try to settle back flat, but if you keep working the surface every 15 minutes, eventually the ripples will stay the way you lifted them.

Building the waterfall

My waterfall is 2" high. First I built up the base with rock castings set into Gypsolite, placing the rocks at various angles to look like they had been honed by centuries of rushing water. After painting and weathering them, I glued on a little debris.

Once the glue and paint had dried, I cut thin strips of acetate to match the height of the falls. This was window material that had found its way into the scrap box. Next, I dabbed five-minute epoxy to the top and bottom of the falls. While it still was soft I inserted the acetate strips, aligning them so they were straight up and down.

After the epoxy had dried, I lightly colored the strips with white paint to look like the air trapped in rushing water. I applied a second layer of five-minute epoxy over the acetate strips to seal them and give shape to the falling water. Using Polly S Reefer White, I drybrushed wisps from the top to the bottom. This was covered with another layer of five-minute epoxy dabbed on with a toothpick.

Next month our subject will be building structures. Here's a shot taken in downtown St. Andrews. to whet your appetite.

────────────

When pouring the water I let the Enviro-Tex Lite run down over the waterfall, coaxing it a little in the right direction with the stirring stick. Just like real water, the epoxy will find the natural course, creating pools and mini-falls.

Once the Enviro-Tex Lite got to the tacky stage, I pulled wisps from a cotton ball and added them to the base of the falls. I pushed the cotton into the epoxy with tweezers, then pulled it away, leaving thin strands standing straight up. The cotton looks like the fine spray created by the falling water crashing on the rocks. This is a little trick I stole from George Sellios.

Next month we'll conclude this series with an article on building structures. See you then. ☖

Adding homes and businesses
to finish our
Pennsy layout

BY DAVE FRARY
PHOTOS BY THE AUTHOR

This month we'll conclude our series on building an HO scale layout with a discussion of the structures. Our prototype, the Pennsylvania RR, was a major coal hauler so I wanted a coal mine to be the center of activity on the layout.

My first step was to make a cardboard template of the mine site. On this template I built a cardboard mockup, which I used to evaluate the size and the height of the mine. I wanted it to fit the space, but not overpower it.

With mock-up and template in hand, I paid a visit to my friend Pete Laier, model railroader as well as an occasional professional model builder. I was running out of time on this project and needed the model built quickly. Pete said he could do it.

Together we searched through the Walthers catalog and several hobby shops to purchase the main ingredients (listed in the bill of materials).

Building the tipple

Pete made the concrete foundation from a Model Power Blue Coal Depot, cutting away the top. See fig. 1.

For the new tipple Pete built a box from .060" styrene, following the profile of the Muir Models Berlin Mills Mine. He coated the box with contact cement and attached the scribed siding. The Muir Models kit is no longer available, but you can come close following the drawings included in fig. 1.

Two girders, swiped from a Walthers overhead crane kit, were used for the incline running into the mine.

Pete cut the roof from .040" styrene

and covered it with Evergreen "corrugated metal" plastic siding. The plastic windows and doors were scavenged from the scrap box, and the lighting fixtures and roof ventilators came from several Campbell kits.

He built the two small sheds at the mine head and the decking along the front of the building from Northeastern scribed siding. The stairway connecting the deck to the ground was made from a Central Valley stairs kit.

Pete built the elevator building from Evergreen corrugated metal, bracing the corners with 1/8"-square styrene. The elevator door was a short piece of fence from a Central Valley fencing and handrail assortment.

The long, low conveyor house spanning the tracks was scratchbuilt from .060" styrene and covered with scale 4 x 8-foot sheets of Campbell's corrugated aluminum siding attached with contact cement. The supporting legs or bents are from an old plastic trestle kit and were trimmed to fit. You could easily scratchbuild some. The dump doors on the bottom of the conveyor house were cut from the bottoms of several old Athearn hopper cars.

Unless you're blessed with a superb scrap box, it's not likely you can build a mine exactly like Pete's. Don't be afraid to modify, using whatever materials and details you have on hand or can find. Real mine builders often did the same.

Auxiliary mine buildings

From our research we found that a coal mine needed a variety of service

Foam core bases keep our buildings level

buildings to operate efficiently. These included a blacksmith shop, battery house, storage building, office, and most important, powerhouse. Its coal-fired boilers made steam for heat and generating electricity.

We wanted the powerhouse to look sturdy and well built, so Pete took the center section of a brick Pola brewery kit and reduced its size so it would fit between the track and the hillside. He discarded the kit roof and added a styrene roof covered with strips of tissue paper "rolled roofing" bonded to the styrene with two coats of Floquil

110013 Grimy Black brushed over the tissue paper.

Rather than paint the brick building, Pete covered it with white tube-type oil paint applied with a toothbrush. He wiped the excess from the surface, leaving filled mortar lines behind.

The steam and compressed air pipes from the powerhouse to the mine were cut from pipe sections found in the Walthers Interstate Fuel kit. The pipe supports are painters' ladders taken from the Central Valley stairs, ladders, and railings kit.

At some mine sites the dynamite was stored in a boxcar so it could be rolled out of the way in case of fire. Instead, Pete elected to build a dynamite house, storage and supply shed all in one. He used the quonset hut included in a Walthers Interstate Fuel kit. I placed the structure behind the mine, and you have to look hard in the photos to see it.

Painting the mine buildings

Pete began by priming all the tipple subassemblies, using a spray can of Floquil 130009 Primer. After permitting this to dry for several days, he brush-

To build a convincing model our author consulted coal mine articles in MODEL RAILROADER and other model railroading magazines before planning this mine. He also looked through some coal mining books at the public library.

---

painted the concrete base with Polly S 500305 Battleship Gray.

He airbrushed the top of the tipple with Floquil 110070 Roof Brown. All the windows and doors in the tipple and outbuildings were sprayed with Floquil 110025 Tuscan Red and allowed to dry thoroughly before installation.

Fig. 1. BUILDING THE MINE. Right: The kits used in kitbashing the mine are shown here. **Far right:** Here's the Muir Models tipple atop the Pola base. Dave built up the surrounding area with pieces of 3/16"-thick foam core board.

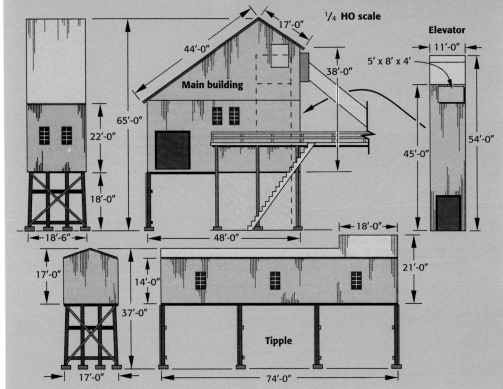

1/4 HO scale

17'-0"

44'-0"

Main building

38'-0"

65'-0"

22'-0"

18'-0"

18'-6"

48'-0"

Elevator

11'-0"

5' x 8' x 4'

54'-0"

45'-0"

18'-0"

17'-0"

14'-0"

37'-0"

21'-0"

Tipple

17'-0"

74'-0"

Bill of materials: Moxie Mine

Central Valley
1601 fencing and handrails
1602 ladders, stairs,
and railways

Evergreen Scale Models
4525 corrugated
metal (plastic)
19060 .060" styrene

Model Power
453 Blue Coal Depot

Muir Models
Berlin Mine
(no longer available)

Pola
806 brewery

Fig. 2. BUILDING SITES. All the structures placed in hilly country were mounted on a level piece of 3/16"-thick foam core board. Dave cut a hole in the scenery shell and then shimmed the base with cardboard to level it. The foam core was held in place with a bead of Liquid Nails.

The corrugated siding and roofing were sprayed with a Tru-Test "Close-to-Chrome" aluminum spray enamel, available at Tru-Test hardware stores. When it had dried, a spray of Testor's 1160 Dullcote killed the shine and provided "tooth" for the weathering. Pete lightly brushed portions of the roof with straight Floquil 110001 Dio-Sol to remove some of the chrome color and blend it with the primer underneath.

Weathering the mine buildings

The job of weathering fell to me. The thing that impressed me most about the coal mine photos I saw while doing my research was the overpowering griminess. Every color was covered with a veil of black.

Step one in weathering was mixing very thin washes of Polly S 410073 Rust, 410081 Earth, and 410013 Grimy Black. I put several drops of paint in a dish and added a squirt of liquid dishwashing detergent and several drops of water. The detergent served as the

"vehicle," with just enough water to allow easy brushing. I stirred the wash until small bubbles appeared and then brushed it onto the buildings, working up and down. Rain washes dirt down, not sideways.

I mixed different shades of the three basic colors on the brush and streaked them on the buildings. Additional full-strength Rust and Grimy Black were streaked under the roof ventilators and around the top of the chimney.

The larger than usual amount of liquid detergent added to these Polly S washes caused the building sides to have a slight "tack" or stickiness, perfect for holding the chalk dust I was about to apply.

I made my chalk powder by rubbing black, rust, and earth-colored chalk sticks over a file. Then I applied them with a large, soft brush, dusting away any excess with an old shaving brush. The chalk stuck to the detergent and produced a dull surface that would withstand handling.

Fig. 3. BUILDING STRUCTURES ON BASES. Above left: Dave built the Thermal King Boiler Co. at the workbench, then mounted it on a sheet of Styrofoam. **Above:** He cut a hole in layout section 6 to accommodate the structure. **Left:** Here's the structure as seen from the opposite side of section 6. Note that work on section 5 is barely under way.

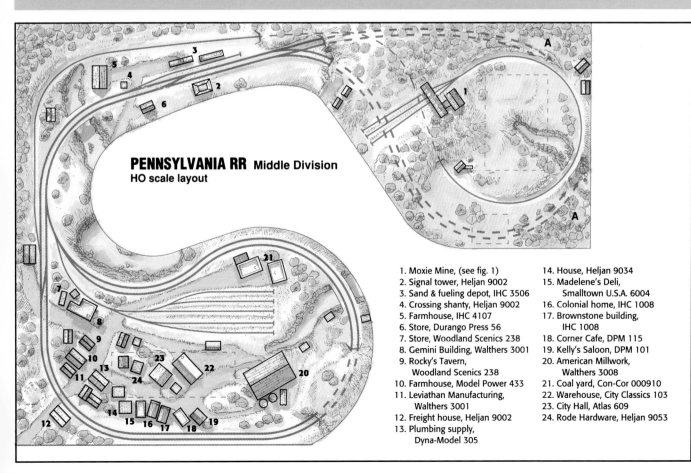

PENNSYLVANIA RR Middle Division
HO scale layout

1. Moxie Mine, (see fig. 1)
2. Signal tower, Heljan 9002
3. Sand & fueling depot, IHC 3506
4. Crossing shanty, Heljan 9002
5. Farmhouse, IHC 4107
6. Store, Durango Press 56
7. Store, Woodland Scenics 238
8. Gemini Building, Walthers 3001
9. Rocky's Tavern, Woodland Scenics 238
10. Farmhouse, Model Power 433
11. Leviathan Manufacturing, Walthers 3001
12. Freight house, Heljan 9002
13. Plumbing supply, Dyna-Model 305
14. House, Heljan 9034
15. Madelene's Deli, Smalltown U.S.A. 6004
16. Colonial home, IHC 1008
17. Brownstone building, IHC 1008
18. Corner Cafe, DPM 115
19. Kelly's Saloon, DPM 101
20. American Millwork, Walthers 3008
21. Coal yard, Con-Cor 000910
22. Warehouse, City Classics 103
23. City Hall, Atlas 609
24. Rode Hardware, Heljan 9053

Selecting the other structure kits

All the structures selected for this layout are kits that looked like structures I saw while driving through central Pennsylvania. Figures 2, 3, and 4 show how I installed them. The track plan lists the major kits used.

Some of the shacks and shanties came from my scrap box, and, frankly, I haven't a clue on the origins of some. Lots of small buildings are available that you can substitute.

The larger towns I visited in Pennsylvania all had several blocks of downtown buildings that had a distinct European styling and were probably built by German or Dutch immigrants in the late 1800s. Hand-cut stone and red brick were the building materials of preference.

The rural areas looked like those I've seen in every other part of the country. Typical was the solitary white farmhouse alongside its red barn, sitting like an oasis in the middle of gently rolling fields.

Many of the towns I visited had seen better days. Their heyday was the late 1940s and early '50s, when America was rebuilding after the Second World War and the demand for coal was high.

So the models on this layout were built and aged to depict middle-aged, middle-class structures, most in fairly good repair, but dirty from generations of coal dust and sooty smoke.

Painting the plastic structure kits

For all kits I followed a four-step painting sequence.

• First, I laid the pieces on posterboard. Then I sprayed them with Floquil Primer, 130081 Earth, or 130082

Concrete. I primed several kits at once, each on its own cardboard square so the parts didn't get mixed. I allowed the primer to dry for several days, aiding the drying process with a small fan.

• Second, I brush-painted the castings with the Polly S colors, placed them back on their cardboard squares, and allowed them to dry overnight.

• Third, I flowed a black wash (1/2 teaspoon lamp black dissolved in 16 ounces of mineral spirits) onto all the pieces. This flowed into the cracks and crevices, slightly darkening the color as it dried and creating a shadow effect. I placed some of the castings upside down so very dark shadows would be created under the larger projections. If you try this, be careful with the mineral spirits. It will remove the paint if it hasn't dried thoroughly.

• Fourth, I let the black wash dry for several days, then lightly dry-brushed all the raised areas with Polly S 410011 Reefer White. This really makes the details pop out.

Finishing the Structures

I assembled the plastic structures using Microscale liquid cement applied with a small brush. Wherever possible I finished and detailed the walls completely before gluing them together. It's just a lot easier to work on them flat at the workbench.

I used Evergreen clear sheet styrene to glaze the windows because it's compatible with Microscale liquid cement and makes a permanent bond to the building walls. The other big advantage over acetate is that clear styrene stays flat. I painted window shades on the interiors of some windows.

Scrap brick and stone from other plastic kits came in handy for making foundations. After painting and weathering them, I glued them to the walls with cyanoacrylate adhesive (CA).

For super-strong joints I applied a bead of baking soda between the building and the foundation and added more CA to make a thick fillet. The CA

is absorbed and bonds immediately with the baking soda to make a hard, almost rock-like joint that's stronger than the plastic.

I used this same technique on the interior corners of the buildings and any other place where extra strength was needed. Anytime you're working with CA you should be careful. Don't

breathe the fumes, and be sure to work in a well-ventilated area.

Every article and every series has to end somewhere, and this one is ending here. I know only a few readers will build the railroad, but I hope lots of you found an idea or a project here that added to your modeling pleasure. See you down the road. ☼

One of the few craftsman kit structures on the layout is the newspaper office from Durango Press. Dave says it reminded him of an abandoned farm near the Juniata River that was surrounded by hundreds of stray cats.

Fig. 4. INSTALLING STRUCTURES. First, left to right: Dave leveled this interlocking tower with scraps of Styrofoam and cemented it to the layout with Elmer's white glue. **Second:** He built up the area by applying Sculpta-mold with a trowel. **Third:** Next came earth-colored latex paint and ground foam for grass. **Fourth:** Dave bonded the materials with a squirt of dilute matte medium. He covered the road with coal cinders and dust gathered from an abandoned mine in Pennsylvania.

Mine Run

1. Just beyond the interlocking tower at Knob Junction, a Pennsy 2-8-0 H9 Consolidation with a cut of empties in tow begins the day with a trot up Gobblers Knob.

2. In no time at all, the train clears Knob Tunnel and starts to work into the hill. At this speed, the engineer seems determined to prove that no. 1493 is no turkey!

3. As the train climbs up the branch line, the bankrupt Gobbler Mine and an abandoned farm can testify to the hard times in the region. But on the Pennsylvania Railroad, not even the deep valleys, step grades, and sharp curves found throughout the Middle Division can slow the pace of operations.

4. In contrast to the meandering waters of Turkey Run, the trip up to Moxie Mine is quick and direct.

Rules of the Road

5. Back in the small mining community of St. Andrews, activity on the downtown streets and the railroad seems to be equally busy. However, as an Alco RSD-5 rolls to a stop on the grade crossing, it's clear who controls the traffic in this part of town.

6. The squealing brakes and idling diesel of the local freight are enough to send a flock of sparrows into flight. But from a bird's eye view, you can catch a glimpse of the real king of the road. Though only for a moment, the freight train must yield to the Pennsylvania Railroad's most important traffic—passenger service.

Standard Fare

7. The bend around St. Andrews reveals that this passenger train isn't much different from other passenger trains on the railroad. Keeping faithful to the "standard," one of Pennsy's 425 K4-class Pacifics runs with a few common P70-class coaches.

8. Now on the outskirts of town, the train races across the Deer Run Bridge and approaches the darkened Summer Ridge Tunnel, one of many tunnels that honeycomb the colorful landscape of the Pennsylvania Railroad's Middle Division.

The Heart of the Pennsylvania Railroad

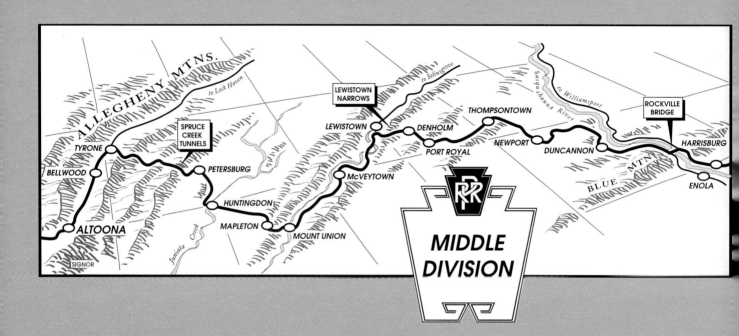

The mighty Pennsylvania Railroad was the dominant member of the American railroad family in its heyday. Its vast network served 13 states, but the Pennsy's core was the original main line from Philadelphia to Pittsburgh. *Heart of the Pennsylvania Railroad* presents GG1s in the east, freights on the beautiful Middle Division, and PRR's mountain struggle at Horseshoe Curve. By Robert S. McGonigal. 11 x 8½; 128 pages; 120 b&w photos; perfect-bound softcover. #01071 . . . . $18.95

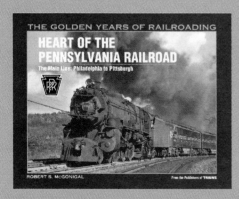